STRENGTH
AND
CONDITIONING
FOR
RUGBY UNION

STRENGTH
AND
CONDITIONING
FOR
RUGBY UNION

JOEL BRANNIGAN

THE CROWOOD PRESS

First published in 2016 by
The Crowood Press Ltd
Ramsbury, Marlborough
Wiltshire SN8 2HR

www.crowood.com

British Library Cataloguing-in-Publication Data
A catalogue record for this book is available from the British Library.

ISBN 978 1 78500 084 3

Dedication
This book is dedicated to those who helped shape my own physical education, and those who helped drive my career. There will always be a debt of gratitude to Ken Bowes, Chris Davy, Ken MacEwen and Jared Deacon. Thank you

Typeset by Servis Filmsetting Ltd, Stockport, Cheshire
Printed and bound in India by Replika Press Pvt Ltd

CONTENTS

INTRODUCTION

Rugby union as a sport has seen continual evolvement over the years, and never more so than since the game officially took its professional status in the higher echelons from 1995. While on the pitch tactics have seen more formalized approaches to skill acquisition, it is probably off the pitch where the biggest changes have occurred. From merely training twice a week on the pitch at schools and clubs, modern day rugby players now train as much off the field of play as on it. No area has developed more than strength and conditioning. The distinct factors that make up the complete rugby player – strength, speed, power, fitness and agility – are now specifically targeted to allow individuals and teams gain the upper hand on the opposition. Players have gone from traditionally training for 'fitness' as an add-on to their rugby training to seeking out structured athletic training interventions. Alongside this, with the modern players being physically bigger and faster, the need to ensure players are more robust and free from injury has led to the demand for knowledge in the prescription of strength and conditioning.

This book lays out the underpinning science of strength and conditioning in rugby. Using the fundamental principles of training, it details a structure of assessing rugby players that in turn will allow appropriate training interventions to be both planned and, most importantly, coached to a wide range of rugby playing levels.

Three distinct 'Case-study Rugby Players' are used to show variation in programming in the applied setting. It's important to understand that while all three are playing the same game of rugby union, the game itself and the players vary greatly in their appearance, needs and subsequent training goals. The examples will allow coaches, parents and players to prescribe appropriate training strategies with specific groups, and review the success of these programmes with objective training data. It is this skill that can be the difference between a player developing and reaching goals within a programme, or ultimately wasting valuable time and energy on an unsuitable training programme.

THE YOUNG DEVELOPING RUGBY PLAYER

The athletic needs of the adolescent developing rugby player form the foundation for all future athletic development. This key stage can often be overlooked, with young players simply being given a watered down version of adult programmes. It can also be an area that is often subject to misinformation and a lack of knowledge. It's essential that the distinct hormonal, mechanical and neural windows are trained appropriately during these stages and to ignore them would be detrimental in the long term. Looking not only at the key developmental stages and how to develop them, it will also pay close attention to other practical considerations such as time available, conflicting sporting commitments, available locations and equipment. The aim is to put in place an appropriate long term development programme that is process driven for future success, rather than outcome driven for the short term.

THE AMATEUR 'WEEKEND' RUGBY PLAYER

While often underplayed, there is still both a desire and a need for amateur recreational rugby players to train appropriately. Not only will it aid performance, but crucially it can help develop more robust, injury-free sportspeople. While prescription of exercise may often appear reduced in volume for the recreational player, it should still be aligned with the same underpinning scientific principles. Again many factors can impact on both time available to train and the potential adaptations but there is still plenty of room for development and improved performance.

THE ASPIRING PROFESSIONAL RUGBY PLAYER

At the far end of the spectrum there is now the need to prepare aspirational rugby players both for professional rugby and the higher levels of representative rugby. While the journey into these ranks will mirror the long term development of the young developing rugby player initially, it must then be appropriate to take players to a higher level of athletic development. Both professional and representative structures nowadays have positional norms with regards to physical characteristics and it requires a higher degree of prescription regarding strength and conditioning. Not only should the programme take into consideration the demands of the game at the higher level, but there is the added factor of achieving the upper hand on the both the more physically capable opposition player, and competitors within the players' own squad structure.

1

THE PHYSIOLOGY OF RUGBY UNION

The game of rugby union has undergone significant changes both in its style and appearance since the pre-professional era, resulting in some marked changes in the physiological profile of the modern day player. As players have become larger, leaner and quicker (1, 2), there has been a conscious shift in the study of the physiological aspects of the game to provide efficacy for modern day programming and training methods. As a result, we now see support teams even at amateur levels having evolved from the traditional two-man group of a forwards and backs coach to an all-encompassing interdisciplinary coaching team. We have also seen the introduction of sport science and medicine professionals such as physiotherapists, video analysts, specific skill coaches and conditioning staff, who work together to pinpoint potential areas where athletic development can improve performance and, ultimately, results on the pitch.

While physiological and anthropometrical profiling is nothing new in sport, rugby union has often proved to be a complicated subject area for the simple fact it involves many different positional groups, each with differing profiles. Whereas the profiling and subsequent programming for more streamlined physiological sports such as sprinting, endurance events

and jumping can be more straightforward, the very nature of rugby means we often have to have broader fields, which in turn can make adaptations harder to come by.

Data from both time–motion analysis (TMA) studies and global positioning (GPS) studies have helped build up a picture of the game and enabled us to quantify speeds, locomotive activity and contact, and to position specific events through tracking of collected data. Although these studies can have some limitations such as showing incidence of activity but not its physical extent, they are a useful tool to guide training. It must also be said the tactical skill level of competition, and indeed the psychological impact of game events, cannot be quantified.

Modern day rugby union consists of repeated, high intensity activities generally with short incomplete periods of recovery (3). These efforts place considerable stress on the anaerobic system (both the phosphagen and anaerobic glycolytic systems) but because of the repeated nature of these over the course of an 80min game, the aerobic system is also called upon to facilitate recovery.

Although rugby is a repeated power-based sport, development and adaptations in VO2 max, or maximal oxygen uptake, can have a significant positive affect on overall performance (4). Activities such as sprinting, tackling, rucking, mauling and the static/dynamic strength and power-based activities should help model the off-field strength and conditioning of the modern player. Of the 80 minutes the game lasts, however, the ball is typically only in play for around 30 minutes (5) so we should really be training players specifically to be efficient in their roles, as opposed to programming for mindless volume. Frequent breaks in play and restarts mean the activity profiles of rugby are typified by short peaks of high intensity work interspersed with low level opportunities for recovery.

Likewise, at junior/lower league levels of rugby, where poorer skill levels tend to be prevalent, we will see a far more staccato type of game, reflected in activity profiles. TMA (6) studies suggest when subdividing the players into their forwards and backs units the work:rest ratios are 1:7 and 1:20 respectively. Both multi-directional and intermittent, typical sprint distances tend to be no more than 15–20m and are commonly from a moving start with up to 20 seconds of incomplete recovery (6).

As mentioned previously, it is the positional variations that complicate profiling. There are both forward positional groups (front row, second row and back row) and back positional groups (half-backs, inside and outside backs). Anthropometrically, backs have been shown to be smaller, leaner, faster and more aerobically fit relative to body mass. Forwards, in turn, exhibit higher level of strength and absolute aerobic measures. This anthropometry is undoubtedly shaped by the game demands on these two groups. Although the modern game has seen a levelling out of stature and lean body mass with some modern day backs dwarfing their forward counterparts, studies still show backs cover a greater overall distance in a game with higher running intensities. Forward groups, however, will spend more time in higher intensity static and dynamic

strength-related activities. Overall, forwards complete around 14 per cent high intensity work to 86 per cent low intensity, with backs showing 6 per cent high intensity to 94 per cent low (Deutsch 2007).

Many of the studies carried out have, therefore, started to help us profile the training we prescribe and give credibility in the training methods we use. However, gaining an accurate physiological understanding of the various components of rugby union (strength, speed, power, agility, and endurance) involves a more detailed look at three distinct physiological systems and how they can develop through specific appropriate training methods. The three systems we must define and understand are:

- The neuromuscular system
- The biological energy systems
- The biomechanical system.

Although we will touch on the basic principles here, the later chapters will look more in depth at the adaptations we can see as a result of different training modalities.

THE NEUROMUSCULAR SYSTEM

This consists of both the nerves and the muscles of the body. Working together in harmony, they are responsible for the movement of the body and on an athletic level must be trained appropriately to ensure the most efficient motor patterns and movement. The nervous system is the body's circuit board, the complex message centre that drives our function. While the principles of physiology could fill a whole book in itself, there are some key areas that must be understood with regards to the function of muscle. These are:

- Muscle contraction
- Structure of muscle
- The motor unit and sliding filament theory
- Musculo-tendinous unit

- Fibre types and distribution within muscle
- Rate coding
- Neural inhibition.

Muscle Contraction

Our muscles move and produce force through differing types of muscular contraction. These contractions differ and can be subdivided into dynamic contractions, those which occur with movement, and static contractions, which involve no movement.

Static Contraction	Dynamic Contraction
Isometric	Concentric
	Eccentric
	Stretch shortening cycle

Fig. 1.1 Types of muscular contraction.

Isometric contractions: These occur when there is tension or resistive force that is equal to the strength of contraction in the muscle. As a result, there is no change in muscle length and joint angle. Rugby presents us with a couple of clear examples. For example, post-engagement in a scrummage situation when both teams are both applying (and resisting) maximal pressure but there is little or no movement. Likewise in many mauling scenarios.

Fig. 1.2 Scrum showing an example of isometric contraction.

Concentric contractions: These involve a muscular contraction that is greater than resistive force, resulting in a shortening of the muscle. Again, the scrummage situation pre-engagement would be a good example. A player will have set himself in a flexed position (eccentrically lengthening). On engagement, the player propels himself forward to a point of impact. As all the propulsion is forwards, only the concentric muscle action is used. Another example is accelerating in a sprint start position. The forward propulsive position means the player only has the option to full extension using concentric movements or risk falling flat (see Fig. 1.3).

Eccentric contractions: On the other hand, these occur when the tension created in the muscle is less than the external resistive forces. As a result, the muscle then lengthens. Landing and slowing down type movements should theoretically exhibit high degrees of eccentric tension. Imagine a player doing a squat with a barbell in a gym. As the player descends or lowers in the movement, the quadriceps will lengthen eccentrically. The ascent, on the other hand, sees the reverse as the player's quadriceps shorten concentrically (see Fig. 1.4).

Stretch shortening contractions: These are concerned with plyometric movement. They use all the muscle actions above and make use of the stretch reflex within the body. The stretch shortening cycle will be discussed in depth when we discuss speed, agility and plyos but the contraction involves creating maximum tension in the muscle by creating a rapid stretch. The fast eccentric muscle action is followed immediately by a rapid concentric action. The faster a muscle is forced to lengthen, the greater the force obtained with the resulting contraction. While sport and human movement can give us many examples, it is probably easiest to describe using an elastic band.

Fig. 1.3 Falling start.

Fig. 1.4 Barbell squat.

Elastic band experiment: Hold an elastic band and pull back to a 50 per cent stretch, holding for 3–4 seconds and release, noting how far the band travels. Repeat the process again but increase the stretch and reduce the time the band is held. Release again. Finally, use a maximum stretch and immediate release. Option three should see the band travel furthest as we have not only stored the optimal amount of energy but also released it quickly.

Skeletal muscle will also have differing functions. Movement and force production will happen as a result of muscle falling into one of three following subtypes:

- Agonist – Muscles that cause movement. They are the prime movers
- Antagonist – Muscles that act to resist movement
- Synergist – While not totally causing movements, these muscles assist the agonist.

Structure of Muscle

To understand the function of skeletal muscle we must first understand its physical structure. Muscles and their fibres are formed like a Russian doll. The outer sheath, or epimysium, forms a continuous attachment from the skeletal muscle to the tendon, and eventually the bony process that allows locomotion to happen. Running through the epimysium there are fasciculi, or muscle fibres, that are bundled together in groups of 100 to 150. The larger the muscle, the more fibres will be bundled. For example, a large muscle such as the gluteus maximus will have far more fibres than a small muscle such as those found in the inner ear. The fascisuli are surrounded by a connective tissue, or perimysium, with each individual fibre surrounded by endomysium (*see* Fig. 1.5).

When we consider all these individual elements of muscle, it is important to remember they all function as one long continuous organism. So tension transmitted from any individual cell will transmit to the tendon (7).

Finally, the individual muscle fibres are cylindrical structures made up of thousands of filaments, or myofibrils. These are made up of a 'thick' filament, myosin, and a 'thin' filament called actin. This functional unit of the muscle (8) is called the sarcomere.

The Motor Unit and the Sliding Filament Theory

The motor unit is the motor neuron and all that it innervates (*see* Fig. 1.6) (7). As the motor

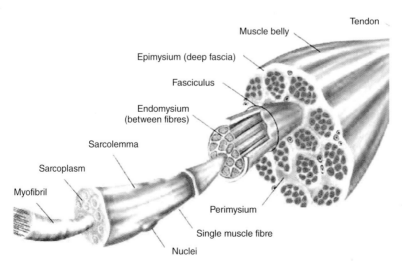

Muscle belly

Tendon

Epimysium (deep fascia)

Fasciculus

Endomysium (between fibres)

Sarcolemma

Sarcoplasm

Myofibril

Perimysium

Single muscle fibre

Nuclei

Fig. 1.5 The sarcomere. (From Cardinale, M., Newton, R., & Nosaka, K. (Eds.) (2011). *Strength and conditioning: biological principles and practical applications*, John Wiley & Sons)

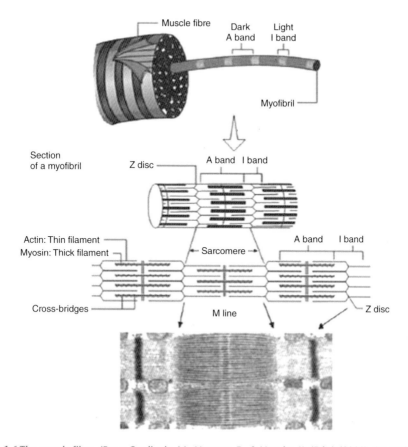

Fig. 1.6 The muscle fibre. (From Cardinale, M., Newton, R., & Nosaka, K. (Eds.) (2011). *Strength and conditioning: biological principles and practical applications,* John Wiley & Sons)

neuron is the command centre for the muscles, the more we can increase the frequency and efficiency of this stimulation, the more we will be able to produce force. When the motor neuron innervates it will transmit to all the muscle fibres within that particular unit. This 'all or none' system means all the fibres innervated in a motor unit must be stimulated, not just some. This makes the motor unit fundamental to all athletic movement and must be considered with our programming. We must look to both increase the number of motor units and the efficiency with which they work. What we train for will determine what we get. Slow static movements will never increase the frequency, thus a player will not get powerful

or reactive as a result. Likewise, if we have a high frequency of innervation but fewer used motor units, we could indeed have a player capable of 'sending the message' to his skeletal structure but not having the force production capabilities.

Central to the innervation of the muscle by the neuron, is a relay centre call the neuromuscular junction (*see* Fig. 1.7). It is here the process of voluntary muscle contraction and human movement begins.

The sliding filament theory dictates the contraction of the muscle. The sliding inward of actin filaments from the ends of the sarcomere on to the myosin filaments causes a shortening of the muscle and in turn a contraction. It is

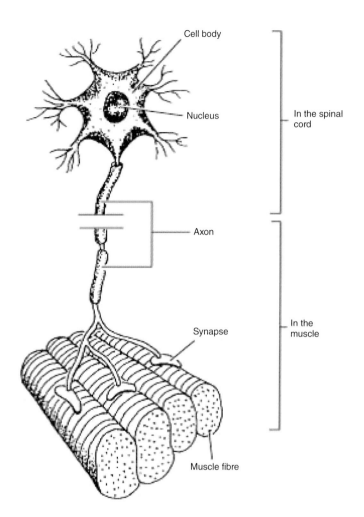

Cell body

Nucleus

Axon

Synapse

Muscle fibre

In the spinal cord

In the muscle

Fig. 1.7 The neuro-muscular junction. (From Cardinale, M., Newton, R., & Nosaka, K. (Eds.) (2011). *Strength and conditioning: biological principles and practical applications*, John Wiley & Sons)

this muscle contraction that allows our muscles to produce force, move or resist movement. The number of myosin cross bridges that attach to the actin filaments, the more force that the muscle will be able to produce. The greater the magnitude and quicker this can be produced, the greater the advantage in sporting situations.

In its normal resting state there is little calcium present in the myofibril, meaning there is little opportunity for binding between the myosin and actin. The thick myosin filaments are characterized by two globular heads that are capable of moving both forwards and backwards in order to bind with the thin actin filaments. The thin filament site consists of actin and two other molecules, tropomyosin and troponin. The actin molecules are supported by tropomyosin and troponin to create a perfect binding site for the globular head of the thick filament.

Once calcium ions are released from the sarcoplasmic reticulum they bind with the troponin and act as a catalyst with the tropomyosin molecules. The amount of calcium released by the sarcoplasmic reticulum is actually what regulates the frequency of contractions (rate coding). This primes the binding site, allowing the thick and thin filaments to attach and in turn allow contraction to take place. This

Fig. 1.8 The sliding filament theory and its six processes.

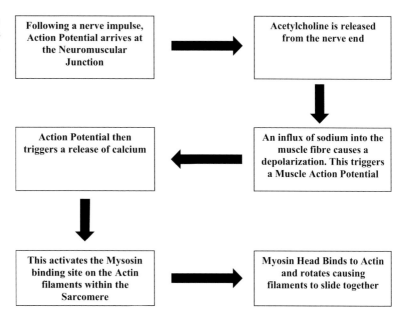

Following a nerve impulse, Action Potential arrives at the Neuromuscular Junction	Acetylcholine is released from the nerve end
Action Potential then triggers a release of calcium	An influx of sodium into the muscle fibre causes a depolarization. This triggers a Muscle Action Potential
This activates the Mysosin binding site on the Actin filaments within the Sarcomere	Myosin Head Binds to Actin and rotates causing filaments to slide together

process happens as a result of breakdown of adenosine triphosphate to adenosine diphosphate and phosphate (7). The catalyst for this is the enzyme myosin Atpase (ATP). It is the regeneration of the ATP that will allow the power output to continue. When there is no longer sufficient ATP to replace the ADP then the voluntary contraction will no longer happen. This occurs in tandem with the calcium ions transported back to the sarcoplasmic reticulum. The muscle contraction is fundamental to our movement and the more units we can recruit, the greater the athletic potential of the rugby player will be (*see* Fig. 1.8).

The Musculo-Tendinous Unit (MTU)

The mechanical muscle complex that harnesses the force production of the motor unit is called the musculo-tendinous unit (Fig. 1.9). It functions through the harmonious relationship of an active contractile component, which moves to create the contraction, and a passive non-contractile component. This arrangement of connective tissues, tendons and ligaments are vital in the release of stored elastic energy.

The MTU structure consists of:

• **Series elastic component** – Primarily tendons and connective tissue that act like a spring. The SEC stores energy as a result

Fig. 1.9 The structure of the musculo-tendinous unit. (Adapted from Hill, 2008 [7])

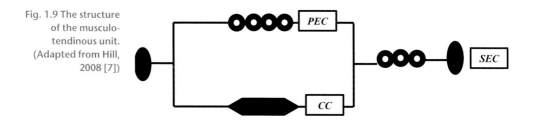

of a rapid stretch within the musculo-tendinous unit

- **Parallel elastic component** – Produces passive force and consists of the epimysium, perimysium and endomysium
- **Contractile component** – This contractile component consists of the actin and myosin cross bridge binding sites.

Fibre Types

A muscle's ability to contract and produce movement is ultimately determined by the proportion of fibre type within that muscle. The fibre type we are born with differs both morphologically and physiologically and should be considered in the programming of rugby players. While there will be a correlation between specific sporting events and fibre profiles (Fig. 1.10), we should also remember an individual's fibre profile when setting athletic goals. Too often the prescription of exercise is misguided in so far as we attempt to programme events and set goals that are physiologically impossible for individuals.

Although studies are equivocal with regards to the number of different fibre profiles with results showing two to eight different types, commonly we concern ourselves with Type 1, Type 2A and Type 2B (*see* Fig. 1.11).

Type 1/slow twitch: These slow oxidative fibres have slow contraction speeds. Used primarily in longer, continuous exercise, they resist fatigue and thus are able to operate for longer time periods. Primarily, they will be used in aerobic activity.

Type 2A/B fast twitch: Fast twitch fibres can be subdivided into being fast oxidative-glycolytic (Type A) and fast glycolytic (Type B). Fast oxidative-glycolytic fibres are fast to contract and are recruited progressively based on how much force we need to produce. They have a moderate ability to resist fatigue and although they are used in general activities, they have a higher energy cost than Type 1 slow twitch. Fast glycolytic are the rapidly contracting fibres reserved for maximal explosive activities. As a result, they are quick to fatigue and require much longer recoveries. They are used primarily for explosive, sprint-based movement.

In the smaller muscles of the body, a single motor unit will consist only of a few fibres. However, large muscles may have hundreds of fibres per motor unit. Function will dictate the fibre make-up of the muscle, with different activities requiring different magnitudes of shortening. If you think of the muscles of the eye, for example, and the speed they are required to contract to blink/move and so on, they are predominantly fast twitch. On the other hand, the deep stabilizing muscles of the midsection are required to work for long periods, do not require such fast contraction speeds and are predominantly slow twitch as a result.

Muscle fibre will also operate under a principle of 'all or none'. When fibres contract they

Sporting Event	Type 1 Fibre Involvement	Type 2 Fibre Involvement
40m sprint	Low	High
Plyometric training	Low	High
Olympic weightlifting	Low	High
10km run	High	Low
80 minutes of rugby	High	High

Fig. 1.10 Correlation of muscle fibre type characteristics and event.

	Type 1 – Slow Twitch	Type 2 – Fast Twitch A	Type 2 – Fast Twitch B
Time taken to contract	Slow	Fast	Very fast
Size of motor neuron	Small	Large	Very large
Ability to resist fatigue	High	Intermediate	Low
Primary activity	Aerobic	LT anaerobic	ST anaerobic
Force production	Low	High	Very high
Mitochondrial Density	High	High	Low
Density of capillary	High	Intermediate	Low
Oxidative ability	High	High	Low
Primary storage fuel	Triglycerides	Cp/glycogen	Cp/glycogen

Fig. 1.11 Physiological characteristics of muscle fibre.

do so completely rather than fractionally. As a result, it is not possible to vary the magnitude of contraction.

Rate Coding

As discussed in athletic terms, how much force we can produce, and the frequency or how quickly we can use it, are two significant differentiators in success. This force production is modulated by both the recruitment of motor units and rate coding. We can produce greater levels of force when more motor units are involved in the contraction, when motor units are increased in size or increasing the rate at which they fire. Rate coding is a time sensitive feedback mechanism that allows low or high frequency of stimulation (9). The central nervous system not only controls how many motor units are recruited but, vitally, the frequency at which they are activated. When doing an explosive, reactive movement such as a sidestep or change of direction we must make sure the body can both call on the required levels of force production and ensure it is done at high speed. Low frequency signalling means the 'machine' (the body) may be

willing, but the 'control system' (the central nervous system) cannot send the signals fast enough. Muscle size will also be a significant driver for the frequency of recruitment. In large muscles frequency tends to be a result of motor unit recruitment, whereas in small muscles frequency is a result of rate coding. As a result, when looking at a physiological basis for training rugby players, it is vital to train both mechanisms. The magnitude of stretch will also affect the frequency of messages sent from the spinal cord. A greater stretch, such as those we will discuss in regard to Olympic weightlifting movements, or plyometric training will in turn lead to increased rate coding.

Neural Inhibition

Strength and the amount of force a rugby player can produce is also affected by levels of neural inhibition. Either conscious or somatic, inhibition can reduce following strength training (10) and facilitate greater levels of force production. Conscious inhibition is the perceptual safety mechanism we all have. It is what protects us from injury and can be both a positive and negative influence on what an individual can do. If you imagine programming an untrained player to bench press 200kg on the first day of training, common sense and intelligence usually prevents him from even attempting to lift the bar from the rack as they know their body will fail under the weight. They have used a conscious process to protect themselves.

The caveat to this is, of course, at times, individuals have to push the realms of what they believe the body can do in order to succeed and develop. Somatic inhibition, on the other hand, refers to the feedback our body receives from intramuscular receptors. Often seen in explosive weightlifting actions and plyometric training, we have to train the body to overcome and disassociate this inhibition in order to allow the movement to occur. In reactive plyometric work such as a depth jump, increased or high levels of neural inhibition will prevent the movement being done with sufficient reactive ability, therefore reducing any potential adaptations.

THE BIOMECHANICAL SYSTEM

While it is often relatively simple to look at training and the body on a physiological level, it is also vital that we look with regards to the biomechanics of training. Key biomechanical factors affecting the human body are:

- Laws of motion
- The lever system
- Muscle cross sectional area and muscle architecture
- Muscle length tension relationship.

Laws of Motion

The human musculo-skeletal system is actually designed for speed and range of motion rather than out and out force production. However, our training often has to find a compromise between these two in order to excel. The force

and power that we can produce are a direct result of the synergy between both the muscle, neural, tendon and bone structures of the body. Fundamental to these are Newton's laws of motion. They dictate not only what occurs to the body biomechanically but also due to external factors such as training equipment and opposing players.

The three laws are:

The Law of Inertia

An object will remain at rest unless acted upon by another external force. Once moving it will remain on this path unless acted upon by an external force or inertia. For example, a weightlifter when starting the first pull from the floor of a power clean must overcome the inertia of the bar and weight to get the bar moving. As he overcomes this inertia the bar will start to move at an increased speed.

The Law of Acceleration

If an object is acted upon by an external force the amount the object moves is directly proportional to the mass of the object and occurs in the same direction. Force is equal to mass multiplied by acceleration ($F = ma$). If we use the weightlifting analogy again, once the weightlifter gets the bar moving it will only continue rising for a short distance (relative to its mass) before gravity brings it crashing back to earth. It is at that point that the lifter must snap under the bar and catch in a low position.

The Law of Reaction

For every action there is an equal or opposite reaction. When force is applied to an object it pushes back against in the opposite direction of the force. If we think of a person jumping, what they are doing is pushing down hard through the floor. It is the reaction of the immovable floor opposing this force that then launches a person vertically.

Effective programming and coaching will not only take these laws into account but also look to exploit them as much as possible in

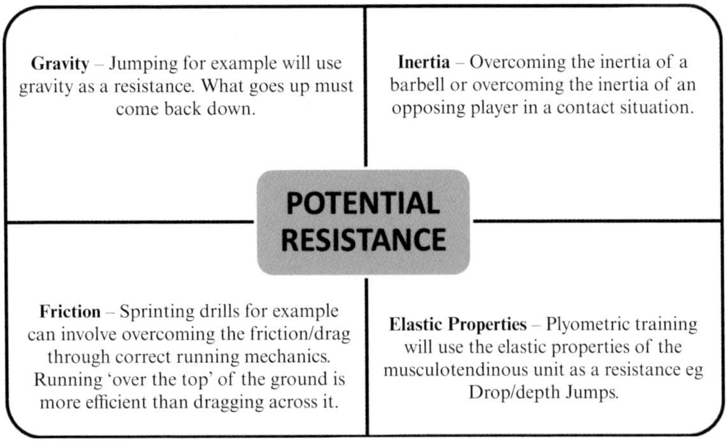

Fig. 1.12 Different types of external resistance.

Gravity – Jumping for example will use gravity as a resistance. What goes up must come back down.

Inertia – Overcoming the inertia of a barbell or overcoming the inertia of an opposing player in a contact situation.

POTENTIAL RESISTANCE

Friction – Sprinting drills for example can involve overcoming the friction/drag through correct running mechanics. Running 'over the top' of the ground is more efficient than dragging across it.

Elastic Properties – Plyometric training will use the elastic properties of the musculotendinous unit as a resistance eg Drop/depth Jumps.

order to yield the greatest responses and adaptations. We generally talk about the production of force in direct relation to overcoming resistance, whether or not it is an external source or something directly related to the structures of the body. But what exactly do we mean by resistance? It is too easy to see resistance as being the weight a person may lift or push but to do so creates a one-dimensional picture. There are four main areas of potential resistance that training should look to exploit (Fig. 1.12) (11).

It is only when rugby players train all these areas that we can begin to get a balanced athletic player who can use the human body to its full potential.

Planes of Motion

Biomechanically we also need to not only understand the body's planes of movement but how they translate to rugby. Rugby, as with most ground-based sport, is multi-directional in nature and requires the player to move in three distinct planes of movement.

The Frontal Plane
The frontal plane cuts the body in half into an anterior (front) and posterior (back) plane. The example shows the frontal plane in motion in a lateral raise exercise.

Fig. 1.13 Frontal plane.

Fig. 1.14 Sagittal plane.

Fig. 1.15 Transverse plane.

The Sagittal Plane

The sagittal plane again cuts the body in half but bilaterally with a right and left side. A lunge pattern, for example, shows the player moving through the sagittal plane.

The Transverse Plane

The transverse plane is any line that will divide the body into an upper and lower section. If someone was to cut a line through the body leaving an upper and lower section we could see the transverse. Fundamental to rotation type movements, the example shows the player moving through the transverse plane in a barbell rotation.

An appropriate training programme and exercise selection will take all these movements into account. It is also true that rugby specific skills often break down when players are contraindicated in these areas. Players with poor passing technique are often affected by poor mobility in the transverse plane, for example. An inability to rotate fully around the lumbar and thoracic spine results in players lacking accuracy when passing both right and left and, likewise, a lack of strength and control in the sagittal plane can lead to poor movement mechanics.

Levers

The body as a machine acts through a lever system as a means of generating movement. As a contraction creates force, the muscle pulls on the bone and creates a rotational pull around the joint. This facilitates movement. The lever system of the body can be catergorized into first, second and third class levers. All levers have three key components and we can use a helpful acronym of FRE (12):

F   A fulcrum such as a pivot or a joint
R   A point or force application against resistance
E   A muscle attachment, where we have a point of application of muscle force.

Muscle Cross Sectional Area and Muscle Architecture

It is the cross sectional area of muscle that dictates how much potential force it can actually produce (13) rather than the volume of the muscle. The greater the cross sectional area of a muscle, the greater the likelihood there will be of a high number of actin and myosin binding

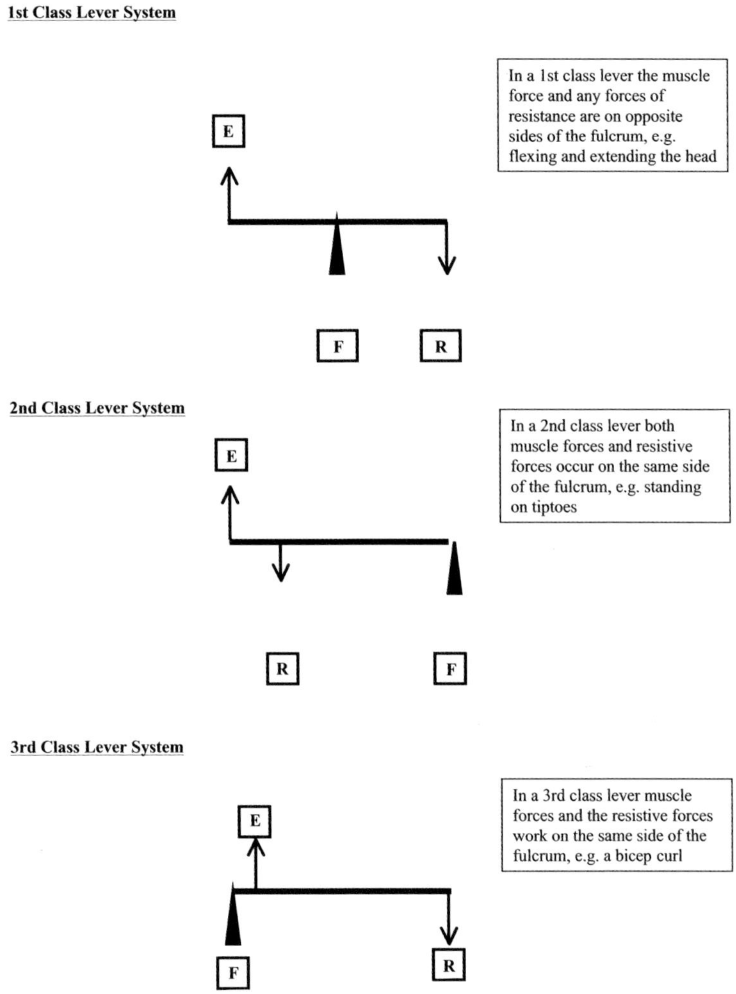

Fig. 1.16 First, second and third class levers.

1st Class Lever System

In a 1st class lever the muscle force and any forces of resistance are on opposite sides of the fulcrum, e.g. flexing and extending the head

2nd Class Lever System

In a 2nd class lever both muscle forces and resistive forces occur on the same side of the fulcrum, e.g. standing on tiptoes

3rd Class Lever System

In a 3rd class lever muscle forces and the resistive forces work on the same side of the fulcrum, e.g. a bicep curl

sites. The more the increased potential for binding (and muscle contraction), the greater the increased potential for athletic development. A good example of this is when athletes follow more hypertrophy-based programmes, designed with bodybuilding in mind. Although they yield good results in terms of increasing the size of muscles, we do not necessarily see the same results in the amount of force being produced. An Olympic weightlifter, on the other hand, while not always exhibiting significant all-over muscle volume (there is certainly a hypertrophy of muscle in key areas), has the ability to produce very high levels of force and call upon that force very quickly. They train specifically for increasing the cross sectional area as opposed to the volume of muscle. Rugby will, however, throw up some interesting scenarios that will be needed to guide the specificity of our training. While creating 'bodybuilder' type physiques may not have sound physiological efficacy, there are going to be occasions when this is necessary in some way. Increased hypertrophy of the upper back, anterior deltoids and biceps, for example, are vital to protect from the impacts associated

Parallel/Fusiform Fibre Arrangement	Pennate Fibre Arrangement
The fibres run parallel to the tendon at origin and insertion. They tend to be long in length and have high potential for shortening as well as velocity of shortening	The fibres run obliquely to the tendon and because of this have an increased number of fibres packed in. They have the ability to produce high levels of force

Fig. 1.17 Types of muscle fibre arrangement.

with carrying the ball into contact and thus need to be considered.

So what exactly affects the cross sectional area of a muscle? The architecture of a muscle plays a vital role in creating an optimum cross sectional area. More importantly, it is the 'angle of pennation' that will dictate the potential results of the contraction. The angle of pennation is the angle between the muscle fibres and the line between the muscle's origin and insertion points (7). The muscle fibres are arranged either in parallel or in a pennate arrangement with an arrow-like or feathered appearance. While more pennate structures promote a greater force production, the parallel fibre arrangements help to facilitate them (see Fig. 1.7).

Many of the larger, prime mover muscles have their fibres inserted obliquely in a pennate arrangement (8). It is because of this that more fibres can be packed in, increasing the effective muscle cross sectional area. The greater the effective cross sectional area, the greater the number of sarcomeres running parallel to each other, increasing the likelihood of cross bridge binding. Also, when the pennate fibres shorten, they are able to create rotational torque around the connective tendon attachment.

Muscle Length Tension Relationship

Muscles will produce different levels of force depending on varying length. They have the greatest ability when they are at a resting length and increases in length will be detrimental to force production. We need to operate at an optimum length that allows for maximum

overlap of both actin and myosin. Too great a degree of lengthening or shortening will change the degree of overlap and will be less efficient. This underlines the importance of both technical and postural proficiency of movement in order to operate at the optimum levels of tension within the muscle. However, we can have an increased potential for force when we increase muscle length as a result of the elastic recoil properties of muscle. The challenge for the strength and conditioning coach is to assess how much we manipulate muscle lengths and velocity of movement in order to be specific to both rugby-based movements and individual athletic profiles.

ENERGY SYSTEMS AND BIOENERGETICS

We have discussed the physiological and biomechanical factors associated with producing force but what do we actually convert this energy into? Ultimately, rugby union requires us to harness our locomotive capacities and convert the energy resulting from our distinct energy systems into a mechanical movement. Energy, or the ability and capacity to perform work (8), will obviously be a key differentiator in success on the field of play. Understanding how this energy is produced, and how to programme training for the best adaptation, is the difference between mindless training and mindful training. While both will have a cost on the body and its systems, it is only the latter that will see a benefit and positive return on our work.

The energy systems are driven by the food and nutrients we consume that make up our

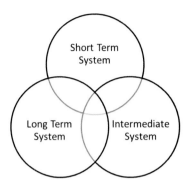

Fig. 1.18 Interplay of metabolic energy systems showing that all systems are working during activity.

individual metabolisms. This metabolism is dictated to by both the catabolic process, or those that break down the stores of the body, and the anabolic process that builds back up. The rate at which these will occur is affected, as mentioned, by the energy we consume or produce and, of course, the intensity and duration of activity. Duration of work will always be inversely related to the intensity of the activity. We cannot operate at our highest levels for long due to the demands they place on the fuel stores, and eventually the structure of our bodies. The training we prescribe will hopefully look to not only increase our ability to replenish energy stores but also to limit the metabolic cost of activity.

The body can operate using one of three energy systems (*see* Fig. 1.8). We have a short term system that allows us to operate at high intensity but only for a short duration and is anaerobic, and so operates without oxygen. It is also known as the phosphagen system. There is also a secondary anaerobic system that operates as an intermediate term process called the glycolytic system. Finally, we have a long term aerobic system called the oxidative system which relies on a continuous supply of oxygen. It is important to remember that, although specific activities and durations will favour a system, they do not work independently of each other. There is a crossover with all the systems working alongside each other at times.

PRESCRIPTION OF EXERCISE BASED ON THE THREE ENERGY SYSTEMS

Effective programming of energy system development in rugby will involve training all three metabolic systems. While the time course of the game is long term, it is populated with intermittent bouts of short and medium term work. The modality of training will be guided, as always, by facilities and equipment that are available.

Speed and agility training – Looking to improve the ability to accelerate, decelerate and change direction
Work Duration – 5–15sec
Rest – 12–20 × longer than work
Repetitions – 10–12
Speed – Maximal or greater

Anaerobic lactate production – To improve anaerobic energy production
Work Duration – 20–45sec
Rest – 3–10 × longer than work
Repetitions – 6–10
Speed – 90–95 per cent

Anaerobic Capacity – Delays the build-up of lactic acid in players
Work Duration – Use intervals of 4-8min
Rest – 1–2min
Repetitions – 8–10
Speed – 75–80 per cent

Anaerobic lactate tolerance – Increase players' ability to cope with lactic acid
Work Duration – 1–2min
Rest – Negative ration, less than work duration
Repetitions – 8–12
Speed – 85–90 per cent

Aerobic Base Training – Improve recovery and endurance
Work Duration – 30min–2hr
Rest – Continuous
Speed – 60–75 per cent

2 | PLANNING AND PERIODIZATION OF TRAINING FOR RUGBY

Once we have established the science behind training athletes, we can now start the process of planning a player's training that will afford us the greatest potential for success, both in athletic training and on the field of play. As a coach, the ability to design and deliver a well-constructed training plan is the difference between being a successful coach and simply being the person who fills time while the players are not training. With time a precious commodity in any of the player groups we train, we want to maximize the effects of our programme to ultimately make a difference to the long-term success of a team. Good programmes delivered by qualified coaches result in positive adaptations. There is a union between the two and if either the programme or the coach is a weak link, then the results will be diminished. There are some exceptional, time-served coaches who have never been able to have athletes realize their potential as a result of poor programming. Likewise, there are some poor coaches who have written great programmes but have then lacked the skills to deliver them and, crucially, adapt them to individuals' skills.

The process of planning can often be a double-edged sword between training not having the required structure to manipulate windows of opportunity or alternatively being a structure too rigid so it does not allow for reactive decisions. A plan should simply be that, a structure that training should follow. It is not a binding document that cannot evolve or react to the many daily challenges of training. Many training plans are written and then must be changed almost immediately. Player injuries, fixture changes and non-selection are just three of the many obstacles that come up. A successful coach must allow for these and adapt a plan accordingly.

As with any other decision process in life, there must above all else be three vital elements. We must plan, execute and, most importantly, there must be a period of reflection. Without this final stage we cannot determine the success of an intervention, nor can we ascertain where refinements are to be made. All experienced coaches will testify to things they have done that have been a success, and likewise things they have done that have not been successful. The simple rule should always be that if something you have introduced as a coach has not had a positive effect on any level (be it physical or psychological), then it would be foolish to carry on with it. With time and experience, we can refine what we do to produce the most superior results. Alongside this as a coach we must also crucially educate, develop and challenge if we want successful, superior rugby players. As this chapter will discuss, how this is done will be generic at the outset but over the training process will lead into a more specific process.

With athletic training, the planning process is termed periodization. Popularized throughout the 1960s and 1970s by Matveyev, Bompa and then latterly by Verkhoshansky, Issurin and Stone, periodization of training is a much discussed and debated area of training. It is the process of dividing the annual training plan of an athlete into smaller systematic phases that allow for both a more manageable training process and, crucially, correct physical peaking for key competitions. By manipulating variables such as volume and intensity, a well-structured plan should look to create a supercompensation of the athletic abilities of players. In short, they should improve, whether it be fitter, stronger and so on. More importantly, by periodizing training there is an ever present need to avoid athletes entering a state of overtraining.

The balance between training hard with tactical and physiological peaks, and 'over cooking' the process is a fine one. However, the damage of the latter can seldom be saved in season. Overtraining can be a state whereby players would start to experience a plateau tactically and physiologically with negative effects on performance. This is incredibly common, and educating and programming your rugby players around the planning process to avoid overtraining will pay dividends later on in the competitive calendar. In rugby, we often see teams peak too early in the season and then go stale at the 'business end' of the competitive calendar. Often a coach can deem a programmed intervention a success wrongly because of its evident supercompensation in a particular training area, such as increased strength or fitness, while in the background the longer-term effects of the intervention could lead to fatigue. It is true that, athletically, the second half of the season is determined by

what is done in the first half and crucially in the off season/pre-season. Remember that by the time the negative effects of overtraining begin, it is often too late to reverse the process. To avoid this we must periodize.

There are several theoretical models of periodization that have been applied through sports over the last few decades and as a coach it is imperative you determine what style will guide your programming. While there is no right or wrong way to plan, there are, as always, some fundamental underpinning scientific principles that must guide us. Two areas guide planning training. There are principles of training and there are variables of training.

- **Principles of training:** Rigid, scientifically proven principles that are set in stone. They do not change, nor evolve, and are simply the eternal laws that govern the effects of training on an athlete.
- **Variables of training:** Variables are exactly that. They can vary and need to be evolved in order to peak.

PRINCIPLES OF TRAINING

Sound, consistent adherence to the scientific fundamentals of training cannot not be understated, if coaches wish to make a successful athlete. Skill-based coaches need also to appreciate the direct correlation between the physical and the skill-based attributes of effective rugby players. The goal is that by having wide ranging physical competencies (and the ability to excel in them), players will have a 'toolbox' to draw upon and help execute technical skills. Over the training journey this should then allow players and coaches to refine these technical qualities so that in the field of play they have greater tactical options. Physical deficiency or being second best physically will always hold back the tactical choices of both players and teams. Rugby is littered with players who are second best through physical inferiority. These range from the obvious areas such as speed and fitness, to the more subtle areas such as players who are one side dominant when stepping or forwards who tire posturally and concede scrum penalties.

Progressive overload: Central to how the body will adapt to training is the general adaptation syndrome (1). It dictates that in any training process following an intervention there will be four distinct processes that occur (*see* Fig. 2.1):

1 Alarm: This is the initial stage where a new stimulus is added. There will be a decrease in performance in response to this. Imagine a strength and conditioning coach working with a team who introduces a training block of higher volumes of metabolic conditioning to combat issues the coach has with players' fitness. This new stimulus will initially cause fatigue as it is an increased stimulus that is above the previous habitual level of the players.

2 Resistance: In response, an adaptation occurs with levels returning to baseline or, in most cases, to above baseline as the players adapt and improve.

3 Supercompensation: As a result of the adaptation there is a new level of performance capacity as players reach new levels.

4 Overtraining: If the training stress is too high, overtraining can occur, resulting in players' performances declining.

Prescription of training must have a magnitude above the habitual level for athletes to develop. At the same time, a coach must keep one eye on the 'long-term lag of training effect' (2). The training process is like investing money. Once an initial deposit is made (training stimulus) there is a time lag before the results of the intervention are seen. This has both positive and negative implications, however. It means in order to reap the benefits of a phase of training we need to be aware of when and how the adaptation will occur. It is no good peaking before a key competition, nor is it any use falling at the last hurdle only for players to be peaking two weeks after a season ends. It is worth noting some of the most successful teams around earn the accolade as year on year they peak at the right time. They may appear off the mark physically early in the season, however they have the ability to

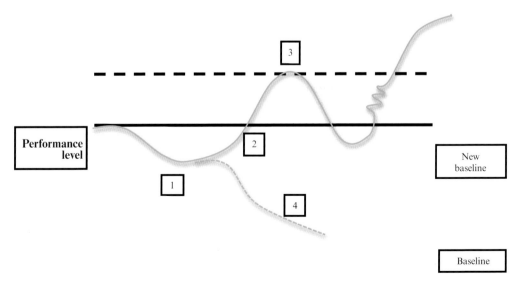

Fig. 2.1 The GAS – general adaptation syndrome.

influence their training so the players are in the best possible shape come kick-off in that final game of the season. The plan must be seen in its entirety as a long-term process.

Accommodation Principle

When training rugby athletes, as with any other sport, we must remember any responses to a training stimulus will decrease over time. Training stimuli become habitual through the training process and thus must be progressively overloaded in order to develop the different characteristics. Players and coaches can sometimes be guilty of continually doing the same training, yet expecting different results. Clichéd as it is, the old saying holds true that if you do what you always did, you will get what you always get.

If a player were to start a programme of resistance training to target upper body strength, for example, they would need to increase the stimulus over time. Programming a youngster three sets of ten press-ups may at the outset yield excellent results and be an appropriate prescription relative to the individual. However, as they gain strength, and indeed a greater neural capacity to carry out the movement, the specifics of load and volume or indeed exercise selection will need to be adapted and progressed. Training must seek to have planned unpredictability in that we want to challenge both mentally and physiologically over time in order to get better. It is important when planning to appreciate that over time a process of diminishing returns will influence training. Early training phases will always give far greater and, indeed, rapid increases in the characteristics you are seeking to train.

Picture training as a continuous line starting at zero per cent. This represents a rugby player with little or no development in any training characteristics such as strength, speed, power and so on. At the other end of that line, 100 per cent, you have your ultimate physical rugby player, a near perfect athletic specimen. The first 80 per cent of that training process can be achieved relatively straightforwardly, through some targeted, underpinned, consistent training. However, the final 20 per cent takes a far more scientific concerted level and often it will seem a lot of work only brings a small amount of change. At this end there are far smaller windows of adaptation and prescribing and delivering training at this point becomes a far more complicated affair. It is a little like when we see 100m sprinters in the Olympics. In the early stages of their career to get those guys running sub 12 and 11 seconds was pretty straightforward once a consistent training regime was put in place, and of course we had someone with a genetic predisposition to the event. However to then run sub 10, sub 9.9, 9.8 seconds and so on coaches need to vary and manipulate more, often only shaving 1000th of a second off a time. However, these marginal increases in speed are what can build to allow a sprinter to run 100th of a second quicker. And that is the difference between being on the rostrum with a medal or being in the stand clapping the winners of the race you just came eighth in. Also, what stage a player is at in his respective training history will impact on what is programmed and when.

Early in the training journey, there are greater gains to be made from training the neural system of a player through various modalities, giving them a 'toolbox' of movement skill. Conversely, with older athletes (with regard to training age) there will be a far greater need for variation.

Reversibility

The human body operates under a 'use it or lose it' principle with regards to athletic development. It is in a constant trade-off between anabolic 'building' adaptations, during periods of consistent training, and catabolic 'breaking' effects once training ceases for too long. Fig. 2.2 shows the timescales within which detraining can occur. With this in mind, successful coaches appreciate the need for training to be cyclical and reflective in order to get the most out of both individual athletes and their training phases. Adaptations to training will only occur in response to prolonged exposure or an intermittent overload in specific areas. These two simple premises are fundamental to athletic development and without them training is merely an operation in work capacity. The need for consistent training is vital to combat reversibility, yet it remains an area where many athletes and, to be honest, coaches fall down.

Consistency of training will yield adaptations. There has to be a consistent measured prescription. If you picture a kitchen sink that has the plug in, the taps can drip over time and in the early stages little happens other than an accumulation of some water. If left, though, over time this accumulation increases and eventually the water will overflow the sink and flood. This is what exercise prescription is seeking to do. If specific training (the dripping tap) is left for long enough there will be an adaptation and subsequent 'overflow' in the physiological

systems. However, what happens if every few hours we remove the plug? The water will run away and then we must start to accumulate again at base level. With this in mind, it is therefore counterproductive for players to take long breaks from training. Certainly in junior rugby and with developing players it is not uncommon for players to reach the end of the competitive season and cease training until the following season resumes. It is little wonder then that development in these early training phases does not occur at the rate many of us desire. Once the training journey starts it really should never cease again until a point whereby a player decides they will no longer chase athletic improvement in rugby. A well-constructed programme will schedule rest but, as shown in Fig. 2.2, it is a very small window.

Specificity

Perhaps one of the most misunderstood principles of training in all sports is the specificity and what exactly constitutes a specific exercise. All too often the prescription of exercises is

ADAPTATION RESPONSE	DETRAINING TIMESCALE	Training Adaptations
Aerobic capacity	3-5 weeks	Training will see an increase in both capillary and mitochondrial density. There will be an increase in aerobic enzymes and glycogen storage
Anaerobic capacity	2-3 weeks	There is an increase in glycogen storage, H+ buffering and anaerobic enzymes
Maximal strength	3-5 weeks	Increases in neural mechanisms and fast twitch myofibrillar density
Strength endurance	1-3 weeks	Increase in slow twitch myofibrillar density, both aerobic and anaerobic enzymes and lactic acid tolerance
Max speed	0-1 week	Increased motor control and neuromuscular function. Also increased phosphocreatine storage

Fig. 2.2 Detraining timescales.

influenced by the assumption that if something looks like the sporting action, then it is more specific and thus will have superior results. However, while some parallels can be drawn between a rugby skill and a chosen exercise it is not enough to simply look at appearance of exercises as your guide. Recent training trends have also seen an influx of 'functional training' methods that appear to be sold as a cure-all for athleticism, yet in reality they are more likely to be counterproductive. As a coach, remember it is your job to both question training methods and, more importantly, create your own rationale for training that has to be based on scientific evidence. We must continually seek a dynamic correspondence between what we prescribe and the desired physiological outcome.

If training does not influence this outcome, then its efficacy and, indeed, validity has to be questioned. Effective methods will be those that deliver the greatest 'transferability of training' (3). There are two distinct parameters where a coach must subdivide specificity. Training must be prescribed and be specific on both a biomechanical level and also a metabolic level. In short, does the training you give your athletes replicate the biomechanical factors that occur with a player in their rugby-related movement, and does it also replicate the metabolic energy system demands of rugby? We can apply the SAID principle in deciding the direction our training should go. This stands for specific adaptation to imposed demands. What we train for is what we get. A simple example would be the metabolic training of sprint/power-based sports and endurance sports. Training a sprinter with long, slow duration activities will not see positive adaptations in the athlete's speed capacity. Likewise, training a marathon runner purely on sprint-based activities is likely to have a pretty insignificant impact on that athlete's ability to use his aerobic system over long periods. There are four main areas we can look at regarding specificity of training (3):

- **Movement specific:** Have you prescribed movement specific training that replicates the key movements of rugby? Rugby is a multi-directional, multi-planar sport that is driven by the ability to move with flexion/extension at ankle, knee and hip. From running, cutting and jumping to contact situations and kicking, rugby fundamentally uses the triple flexion and extension movement in all these actions, and thus this is our rationale to train it. Moreover, these movements occur with two legs in contact with the ground, and more often than not one. With that in mind, we could then say exercise selection that included squat and lunge base patterns would have efficacy as a training method.

- **Direction of force production:** As mentioned above, in order to move horizontally, vertically or laterally a player must impart force into the ground. Without this no acceleration or movement can occur so it is important we train in a manner that allows us to use directing force through the floor.

- **The amount of force needed:** Positional differences mean different levels of force production are required at different times so there is an element of individualization in players' training programmes to reflect this. If you look at the force demands of a contact situation, we have high levels of force exerted. On the other side if we have a player changing direction with a sidestep at high speed then lower levels of force are required (albeit imparted into the ground quickly).

- **The rate of force:** As above, players are required to call upon force production at different rates. Using the example above, the maul will have very high levels of force production but a low rate at which they are produced. The change of direction, on the other hand, will lower levels of absolute force but the neural system has to call on them very quickly so the movement is done explosively and reactively.

Recovery

The final piece of the jigsaw with regards to the planning process is the principle of recovery. The human body does not improve in a constant linear fashion. As seen with the general adaptation syndrome (GAS), in order to supercompensate physiologically there has to be a restorative period following a new training impetus that is above the habitual level. If this were not the case a player could start a strength programme and continue without fatigue, experiencing constant increasing adaptations. Sadly this is not the case otherwise we would be dealing with some of the athletic elite! An effective programme involves the manipulation of volume and intensity stimuli with a view to exploiting the GAS. By doing this we can reduce fatigue and monotony and have players peak when we want them to. This balancing act between work and rest will result in physically and mentally sharp athletes.

It is important, however, to stress fatigue in itself is not a bad thing. We will always have fatigue after a new training phase. It is a naturally occurring adaptation in the body that signals work at a level above that which was previously accommodated. And thus, with intelligent restoration and recuperation, it is the springboard for athletic development. A significant imbalance between training and recovery, though, will result in one of three negative situations.

Firstly, staleness and monotony occur when players are not appropriately challenged and stimulated on both a physical and psychological level. It can be commonplace in many team sports and its avoidance is a result not only of effective recovery in programming but also the cooperation of skill coaches in order to maximize the fuel players have in the tank. The nature of a rugby season sees not only a high volume competitive schedule but also the demands physically of training, playing and injury. This means multi-disciplinary cooperation and communication is core to managing players' recovery levels.

Secondly, we want to avoid the debilitating effects of overtraining and overreaching. Overreaching will see short-term increases in training volume and intensity that result in short-term decrease in performance. While commonplace following specific intense training blocks such as increased metabolic conditioning or speed work, the timing specifically of the recovery phase to bring about a subsequent positive increase in athleticism is paramount. While players may get away with mild fatigue in minor games, it is not going to be very successful if players approach big games in poor physical and mental condition.

Over a longer time, of course, overtraining will bring about a tactical, physiological and mental plateau that will affect performance negatively. As this can last weeks into months when it occurs, a strength and conditioning coach must use an informed process a little and try to predict future windows of opportunity for training and potential traps. This is done at the start of the season and then reacted upon throughout the season. It is not a scenario that can be improved drastically in the latter stages of the season because there is simply no longer the time.

VARIABLES OF TRAINING

As mentioned previously, once training is driven by the solid principles of science, a coach can then use variables to manipulate it to elicit the greatest outcome. Once we understand the acute variables of training the content of a training plan can be manipulated to allow adaptations at crucial times in a season. Typically, peaking in rugby can be highlighted as a team wanting to be at its best for cup finals or in the later stages of the season. However, even peaking in the training week and within a game can be used to guide training. Long-term planning will always ask the question of what is the training priority and, more importantly, when do we wish it to happen?

We cannot have everything; trade-offs in training are commonplace. For example, you may want to increase your team's metabolic endurance capabilities through a game. However, you may also wish your team to be bigger, stronger and be capable of greater speed/power 'endurance'. Sadly, the two play off against each other so prioritizing what you programme and when, and whether or not it will complement subsequent training, become key considerations. Adaptations occur best when single (or complementary) training modalities are programmed. Typically, strength and power training sit well together, as do elastic/plyometric and strength training methods. Acute variables allow you to vary and alter the training stimuli and can be:

- **Volume:** Training volume refers to the total amount of work done in a session. This can relate to the programming of sets and reps, the number of foot contacts in plyometric training, the distance moved or the speed moved. It can often be measured as 'volume load', which would be the reps × load, for example, in a strength programme. A player lifting five sets of five repetitions in the back squat may lift sets one to five at a load of 120kg. The volume load of the session would therefore be 3,000kg (5 × (5 × 120)). It is a simple and effective method of assessing training volume and can be useful as a monitoring and predictive tool for performance. Although the case studies will refer in more depth to specific examples, it is worth remembering who you are training when determining volume load. Generally speaking 'trained' individuals will have a higher tolerance than 'untrained' players and are likely to require greater levels of stimuli in order develop athletically. Conversely, older athletes (thirty years and over) often need volume reduced compared with younger players.

- **Intensity:** Exercise intensity is the power output of a movement. Typical ways it may be expressed would be in resistance training, where intensity can be programmed as a percentage of a one repetition maximum. Alternatively, it could be also shown as a wattage output on a cycle ergometer or the stroke rate on a rowing machine. Intensity is inversely proportional to volume, however, so we cannot have a situation of high volumes and high intensities without an appreciation that fatigue, and subsequently a drop-off, can occur. We can increase volume or intensity but not both. Recovery must also be programmed accordingly. Again, the training age and fragility of athletes must be taken into consideration. Developing athletes should not be working at near maximal intensities.

- **Frequency:** The frequency of training is the amount of reoccurring training sessions the athlete is programmed. Volume and intensity are again used in the management of the training frequency as we are always looking to optimize the effects of training with the least fatigue on the body. A common-sense approach should also guide frequency around specific scenarios such as training and chronological age, gender and sport demands. In a contact sport such as rugby recovery from both competition and training throw up different challenges to, say, a racket sport where there is no recovery needed from contact situations. It is also worth noting that, with rugby, skill-based training such as scrummaging, defending and contact will often produce significant fatigue and thus will affect subsequent off-field training and vice versa.

- **Rest/recovery:** The programming in of rest and recovery may refer to intra-set recovery but also recovery throughout the training week and the training year. Late season will see potential fatigue from the accumulation of the rigours of the season. Likewise, training neutrally demanding modalities such as speed will require greater recovery windows.

- **Density:** This relates to how dense any specific session is. While we may have two individuals training in the weight room, the density of their sessions can be vastly different. Player A may have four sets of five reps programmed on five different exercises, seeing a total of 100 reps in a session. Player B may be in for a similar time and may have the same programme but each major exercise may be super-setted with four sets of eight reps on an auxiliary exercise during rest periods. On repetitions alone, player B will do 228 reps in a session yet they have spent the same time in the gym. The question of having dense sessions is a much argued point in that, on the one hand there is a potential for fatigue, which will thus be detrimental to subsequent exercises. On the other hand, the coach who has limited time with his players may be looking to maximize their training time. As long as the exercises chosen as a superset are not fatiguing to the main exercise it can be a useful tool. Often we see prehab/injury prevention type exercises working well here.

- **Training stimuli:** Altering the training stimuli is perhaps the greatest area of variability with regards to structuring training and its subsequent adaptations. Exercise choice, order and movement characteristics will all contribute to the training goal but their potential fatiguing effects must be managed appropriately. Likewise, the configuration of sets and reps and the choice of training equipment should all be taken into consideration.

CREATING THE LONG-TERM PLAN

Once we have determined the logical path to follow in line with the principles of training, it is time to start to flesh out the long-term plan. Ultimately, it will be guided by two major factors: the sport (rugby) and the individual needs of the player. While differing levels of player will play a significant part in this, we have to always start with a thorough needs analysis. This mental map will allow us to determine exactly what methods we can use to achieve our end goal. There can be many combinations of training that can result in success. By deciding on the final destination, such as developing a team to win a championship, we can then start to look back at the factors that will guide us in our planning, remembering, of course, that reflective practice will be integral to a reactive organic plan.

Considerations in planning are not an exact science, with every scenario throwing up different challenges and opportunities, but the following are common:

Training background of individual/team: As we have mentioned, training age does not always match chronological age. A player may have been playing for some time but never have actually trained in a consistent, informed manner. Players with relatively low training backgrounds will need lower volumes and intensities of training for the simple fact they are not yet conditioned to training in a routine, progressive environment. Throw too much at players too early and there is a risk of fatigue, burnout and disillusionment. On the other hand, if you do not expose them to the required stimulus you may find little or no change in their physical characteristics. Generally, players can be classified into novice, intermediate or advanced/elite. Novice or beginner athletes generally have no training background and have never really adhered to a structured, performance-based programme.

They probably make up the majority of players out there in the wider game in that they are often distinguished by recording performance test results that fall into the bottom of the normative data ranges. Intermediate athletes have several years of training experience although it may not necessarily have yielded sufficient performance gains to move up any testing norms. Finally, the advanced or elite athletes are exactly that: they are seen to not only exhibit top end test results but also high skill-based achievements, such as representative selection.

Injury history: Injuries can be both individual, such as an acute soft tissue injury, and global among a squad, such as successive hamstring trauma as a result of poor movement and posterior chain conditioning. Asking why and how injuries have occurred can often help map the direction a plan should take and may sometimes be a result of a high frequency of competitions.

Age: As the case studies will show, age must always be considered. Young athletes should be looking at a more long-term process-driven programme that takes into account their maturation stage and age. Older players, on the other hand, may either need a more outcome-driven plan, such as the older professional player who has a season to see out before retirement. Arguably, the work, both positive and negative, has occurred with this player and thus there is little in the remainder of his playing time that can be altered. The likelihood is that, on some level, the outcome is merely to stay injury-free for the remainder of the season.

Gender: Male and female athletes react differently to different stimuli and have different needs. High prevalence of ACL knee injuries in young women may mean a plan is driven more to the prevention of serious injury. Women also tend to have far less exposure to strength

training so this will always be evident in their programmes. However, it must be said all plans should have injury prevention as a core goal.

Psychological profiles: As with the skill-based side of a sport such as rugby, there will always be a case of a squad exhibiting differing mental attitudes from players. Every squad will have both those players who exhibit a mental resilience for intense work and those who simply cannot tolerate the same levels. While it is easy to write off the latter, a good coach must sometimes alter their approach to cater for the differences among individuals.

Training/competition calendar: The amount of skill-based sessions and games will affect how many strength and conditioning sessions are optimum in a week. Remember, the fatiguing nature of the actual positional skills in rugby mean overtraining and inefficiency in training are always in the back of our minds.

Facility and athlete numbers: Not all clubs have access to the equipment needed for all modalities of training and thus the plan is driven by what you can do best. If you had large numbers, only outdoor space and the only equipment available was sandbags, logs and tyres you could still run effective sessions based around making players fitter, faster and stronger. The situation is limiting but not impossible. As a result, what you do may look different to the next club, however, this does not mean it is any less effective.

Coaches: Finally, and most importantly, how many coaches are available? If you only have one or two coaches and thirty-plus players, don't expect to be able to coach every player individually. You must cut your cloth accordingly and plan interventions based on what you can do most effectively, within your limited environment.

Now we have a deeper understanding of what challenges and constraints we face, the

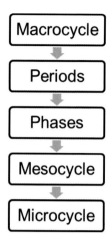

Macrocycle

Periods

Phases

Mesocycle

Microcycle

Fig. 2.3 Subdivided units of periodization.

next part of the planning process is to decide on what specific style or periodization we will use. The concept of subdividing units is not new in training but was popularized in the 1960s when the West became more aware of the practices the Russians and East Germans had been using.

Training in all models of periodization is broken down into distinct units reducing in size, as seen in Fig. 2.3. A little like a Russian doll, all units sit inside the next one up for the effect to work. Incomplete units mean there will be a weakness in the plan. A macrocycle refers to the global longer-term time period such as a season, or a four-year quadrennial cycle that an Olympic athlete may use to plan training. Periods refer to distinct, focused blocks such as competition periods and preparation periods. In rugby, this could be as simple as your pre-season phase and your competition phase being the season itself. These phases can be further broken down into periods of training with general preparation moving towards more a more specific focus. Historically, mesocycles are then the individual training blocks. Although various timescales can be used, it is quite common (although not always) for these to be broken into four-week blocks. Finally, these four-week mesocycles will be subdivided

again into weekly microcycles where variables, as previously mentioned, are used to vary the training effect. Although we have all these different phases, they are all built around periods of development, competition, active recovery, and the repetition and progression.

Traditionally, periodization models are guided by the competition schedule of the sport. Individual sports such as track and field had neat linear models as they had long training periods generally interspersed with a low volume of competitions. A team sport such as rugby, on the other hand, had weekly competitions and thus a more complex non-linear model was required that looked to achieve a minimum number of training units around competition to get a positive training effect.

Matveyev's traditional model consisted of a preparatory period, a competition period and a 'transition' period. In the individual Olympic sports it was designed for it had some solid advantages in so far as it offered athletes long-term exposure and experience in the attainment of different physical characteristics. The preparatory phase that was split into a general preparation phase (GPP) and a specific preparation phase (SPP) ensured athletes had solid initial levels of sport-specific fitness. And as there was a successive model physiologically, subsequent characteristics were potentiated by the phase before. A base of strength endurance or hypertrophy led into strength, which in turn laid a platform for power and, as a result, athletes could potentiate the training of speed.

This traditional model certainly had its advantages, although specifically around its application in single modality sports (endurance-based such as middle distance track events, swimming and so on, and single power events such as shot and discus). It resulted in the athletes gaining deep long-term experience in each phase through this ordered consistent approach. Both the GPP and SPP phases meant there were elevated levels of sport specific fitness that benefited from potentiated adaptations from the preceding phases, both annually and quadrennially in the training cycle. However, this model became constrained in the long competition phases where it saw a reduced potential for maintenance in sport-specific fitness. It was also found that even the top athletes struggled to maintain their 'peaks' for more than three weeks. This meant it was inappropriate in team sports where weekly competition peaks demanded a greater level of undulating peaks.

As a result of these findings and a natural evolution of training methods, newer periodization strategies emerged in the form of Verkhoshansky's Conjugated Successive System, Phase Potentiation popularized by Stone and Block Periodization put forward by Issurin. Both the conjugated method and the block method allowed several qualities to be trained together at once with a single training modality to be emphasized at any one time. Still, with its origins in track and field, there was the assumption that by training a series of concentrated loads there would be positive after-effects from the previous load and they would last a reasonable amount of time. A year would be broken into three stages with two to three training phases. For example, while speed was being emphasized, strength work may recede back into a maintenance phase rather than being abandoned altogether. This method would sit a little better for developing a team sport such as rugby as it assumes numerous competition peaks. If we consider a premiership team, they will often compete on three fronts with distinct times in the year to peak. These may be cup qualification and completion, the league campaign and hopefully the subsequent play-offs or, if they are unlucky, the battle to escape relegation.

Finally, phase potentiation (originating from strength/power sports) based its framework of planning on the assumption that individual physiological qualities cannot be developed for long phases. Likewise, simultaneous training of these could be counterproductive. While strength and power sat well together, as did speed and plyometric training, there was certainly a case that aerobic training was counterproductive to strength increases. Almost identically to CSS and block periodization, it still based its methods on the theory there would be potentiated effects from each phase.

So this leads us to the question of which would be best in an undulating team sport such as rugby? All have their merits and all at times will produce a positive effect. In the untrained, a traditional model will still achieve goals; likewise the latter models would benefit a more trained athlete. However, rugby will always be tricky in that it requires all physical characteristics to be trained. A team that is simply fit and not strong and powerful will not have the physical capability to manage rugby's explosive phases. Similarly, a team of explosive anaerobic players may not have the aerobic engine both to remain effective over 80 minutes and to recover.

It is important we accept models generally derive from nice neat scenarios. So we can take the positives of all systems to help guide a plan. However, a plan is merely that. It is a framework to work to and evolve, not something that is binding and set in stone. It is too simplistic to hold to one plan when weekly competition throws up differing match demands/intensities, injuries and the consequences with regard to physical training. Planning should always have a plan B, plan C and probably a plan D in reserve. Adaptability is the difference between success and failure whether on the pitch or in the planning meetings of backroom staff.

However, there are some guidelines that may help when planning for scenarios such as our case studies.

The Amateur 'Weekend' Rugby Player

With the amateur 'weekend' player the vital thing is to be realistic. Constraints on time and the fact that you may well be inheriting a lifetime of poor training habits mean it is

Pre-season	Gross athleticism Aerobic capacity Strength endurance Mobility	3 × per week generally Tuesday, Thursday and Saturday
Preparation 1	Strength endurance Anaerobic capacity Semi skill-based specificity	2 × per week as part of the overall skill-based session. If appropriate, extra sessions around skills training
Pre-season 2	Gross athleticism Aerobic capacity Strength endurance Mobility	2 × per week
Preparation 2	Strength/power High skill-based specificity	1-2 × per week pre skills training
Peak	Peaking of anaerobic characteristics	1 × per week

Fig. 2.4 Specific content of annual plan for amateur players.

not going to be possible to change the world. The plan must also be very flexible in nature as the realities of working patterns and, at times, commitment levels mean we require a framework rather than a deep intricate plan.

We must always remember what the key goal is, and that has to be injury prevention paired with an increase in gross athleticism. Declining numbers in the junior club scene mean we need to make the most of the players we have, as there is simply not the depth through the ranks. And while time for consistent training is limited, we find significant advances in physical qualities can be made with some simple interventions. While in season there are demands on time, with many clubs training twice a week and seemingly having to fit in a large amount of skill work, one glaring opportunity that links all the case studies is the pre-season period before games begin. There will rarely be the same opportunity for a concentrated focus of physical conditioning again in the season so it is vital the amateur player front-loads his conditioning plan. As the season develops,

invariably numbers drop, the time available to carry out conditioning decreases and matters tend to turn to skill-based training. While we discussed earlier the limitations of a traditional linear style in planning for team sports, there is efficacy in using a structured plan as such where the players focus on single physiological characteristics, as seen in Fig. 2.4.

Generally, players at this level will present with poor all-round conditioning, movement and general strength and these must be the 'go to' areas of development for maximum effect. One point of note with this level must always be that we are not training elite players. The driving force for most, if not all, of these players is still to participate and be successful in a game they enjoy. And while results will always drive any competitive sport, coaches must be acutely aware the training plan must be in part driven by the traditional ethos of their club. It is a fine balance between developing players physically to enable a greater chance of success and overdoing the process somewhat and trying to create elite level players. At the elite end of rugby, approaches can be very much more results-driven and have to be. Training reflects this but the same would not work in clubs where the social aspect of the game is fundamental to success. As with anything, the key is in getting the balance of what science tells us is effective but altering it to be appropriate for our environment.

The Aspiring Professional Player

While planning for aspiring players in a semi-professional or professional set-up should follow a long-term, process-driven approach, the nature of these more elite clubs mean there is often still a more short-term outcome process. The onset of professionalism in rugby has, to an extent, meant at these levels clubs are interested in what can be achieved in the short term. As there tends to be a financial outlay by the club, they often want players who are either a 'finished product' or at best will reach a level in twelve to eighteen months that mean they can be slotted into the senior team. As a result, they tend to take players who have matured early, have some obvious physiological traits or have a certain distinguishing trait over their peers. Invariably, in the modern game this is a physical one, with players often recruited on physical characteristics on the assumption the skill development can be attained relatively easily. And as a result, their season planning reflects this. We often see watered-down planning and programming at academy level that is often not dissimilar to the senior level players. That being said, young aspiring players who have been in programmed athletic development programmes in clubs from a young age and have benefited fully from training the appropriate physical characteristics at the right windows of opportunity will often already be more advanced than their senior counterparts.

The planning process at this level is driven by success in the similar results-based outcomes seen at senior level. The year plan will be well structured as it is more than likely these young players are in a full-time training environment. That means they have the both the time available to train and, more importantly, the time available to recover. The plan is built around developing the individual and the team simultaneously to win games.

As mentioned earlier, with the differing styles of training periodization there will still be key windows to exploit. In my experience, young aspiring players benefit best from a training environment that has a main focus in any one specific block. However, other physical characteristics are still always trained alongside the main focus. The players' stages of maturation and physiology mean they are both receptive and effective, and developing positive adaptations in specific physical characteristics. These are vital training years that will define the types of players they will become. Currently, we see many instances of coaches being too one-dimensional in their physical training as they fall into the trap of chasing the number or test result, rather than being guided by an overall rugby outcome. This is probably seen most in strength development with young men. While strength is fundamental and vital to both their development and success, it must be developed alongside all characteristics. Rugby is littered with stories of the schoolboy international with legendary scores in strength tests who seems to fall by the wayside once he develops into a senior player. As an effective strength and conditioning coach with young players (and all players to some extent) there is a necessity to keep all the plates spinning at one time. If we want all-round, balanced rugby players we cannot afford to work only on one set characteristic. For example, players may well be in a strength or power phase but we must still challenge them in the background with other physical characteristics. As seen previously, many characteristics marry well together and benefit from a potentiated adaptation. Speed and plyometric exercise, for example, or strength and power.

As with any rugby player, the pre-season block for the aspiring professional will be vital. It is still the only really concerted block where players can accumulate the required amount of volume without needing to consider weekly competition. And, as shown previously, what is done in the pre-season will be most evident in the later stages of the year. With that in mind, I would divide my year into:

• Pre-season
• Competition 1
• Competition 2
• Peak.

While the terminology used may reflect other concepts, it is important to remember it is merely that, a term. A phase can be called whatever a coach wants; it is the content and delivery that is important. And, while it will also be guided by the accepted models of periodization, I have found that planning in a multi competition sport such as rugby often blends elements from all models.

Pre-season phase: Provided players have not been on summer tours, nor have they finished the previous season late, I favour a long twelve to thirteen week pre-season block.

While some of this can be self-directed, I have found the level of volume and degree of focus vital to player development. This plan is for players already with two or three years' training history.

It is also important to remember that in weeks nine to twelve there will be the introduction of warm-up fixtures. While vital to the preparations, I feel to a certain extent developing players should 'train through' this process where possible. I think the week should reflect a normal taper as the game approaches but the benefits of this extra four-week block of quality physical training will outweigh the benefits of a drastic reduction in volume. We should always have in the back of our minds that the long-term goal is always to have players in the best possible condition both mentally and physically in the later stages of the competitive season.

Competition phase 1: The first main competition phase consists of roughly three four-week training blocks that should take the player into late December. There will naturally now be a weekly competition focus with players competing in both club and academy games and, as a result, the plan should accommodate this. Players should still hold a training volume but recovery pre- and post-weekly games must be programmed in. We will still see a front-loaded

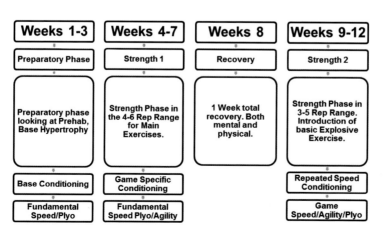

Weeks 1-3	Weeks 4-7	Weeks 8	Weeks 9-12
Preparatory Phase	Strength 1	Recovery	Strength 2
Preparatory phase looking at Prehab, Base Hypertrophy	Strength Phase in the 4-6 Rep Range for Main Exercises.	1 Week total recovery. Both mental and physical.	Strength Phase in 3-5 Rep Range. Introduction of basic Explosive Exercise.
Base Conditioning	Game Specific Conditioning		Repeated Speed Conditioning
Fundamental Speed/Plyo	Fundamental Speed Plyo/Agility		Game Speed/Agility/Plyo

Fig. 2.5 Breakdown of pre-season phase training plan for aspiring professional players.

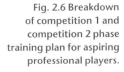

Fig. 2.6 Breakdown of competition 1 and competition 2 phase training plan for aspiring professional players.

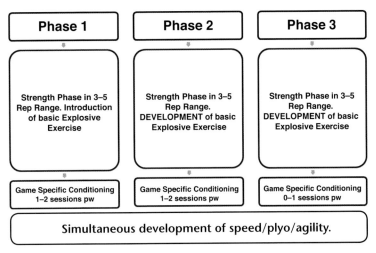

Phase 1	**Phase 2**	**Phase 3**
Strength Phase in 3–5 Rep Range. Introduction of basic Explosive Exercise	Strength Phase in 3–5 Rep Range. DEVELOPMENT of basic Explosive Exercise	Strength Phase in 3–5 Rep Range. DEVELOPMENT of basic Explosive Exercise
Game Specific Conditioning 1–2 sessions pw	Game Specific Conditioning 1–2 sessions pw	Game Specific Conditioning 0–1 sessions pw

Simultaneous development of speed/plyo/agility.

week, meaning volume will be reduced leading into a game.

Competition phase 2: Post-Christmas will see players with roughly a three to five-month run-in to the end of the season. It is now that the benefit of the summer's work will become apparent. Many teams have arrived at this stage in the season and then panicked about players not being in peak condition. While a little reactive work can be done, more often than not the players are starting to be challenged by the accumulation of the season so far and need to be handled carefully. If as a

coach you want your team peaking in the late season, now is not the time to overload with mindless volume.

Specifically, this second competition phase with the aspiring professional will see training develop from general work to building a more specific platform. The solid strength foundation will still remain in a weekly timetable but more in the background. Overall, the strength platform will help the player develop and execute a greater power-based repertoire. Similarly, the intensity of this work will increase, volume will decrease and coaches must apply more reactive programming.

Fig. 2.7 Breakdown of peaking phase training plan for aspiring professional players.

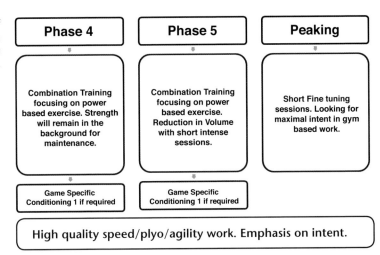

Phase 4	**Phase 5**	**Peaking**
Combination Training focusing on power based exercise. Strength will remain in the background for maintenance.	Combination Training focusing on power based exercise. Reduction in Volume with short intense sessions.	Short Fine tuning sessions. Looking for maximal intent in gym based work.
Game Specific Conditioning 1 if required	Game Specific Conditioning 1 if required	

High quality speed/plyo/agility work. Emphasis on intent.

Peaking: This final peaking stage is often dictated to by the competitive position the players are in. Hopefully, on the back of a successful season, players will be looking to be successful in the latter stages of cup/league competitions and be pushing for summer tours in representative structures. With that in mind, we must be aware of the volume of training and competition already carried out. Players will be getting a little fatigued, regardless of planning. Session volume has to come right down. Often a hard thing for many coaches to give up, training time should be as efficient as possible allowing vital skill-based sessions to take precedence. It is also worth noting at this stage of the season there has to be a certain amount of individualization with regards to making players as confident as possible. There are often grounds to put some sessions in that we know make players 'feel' good. The power of confidence cannot be underestimated. Self-belief has produced, and will continue to produce, situations in sport where the physically inferior still come out on top.

The Young Developing Rugby Player

While Chapter 3 looks in depth at the long-term development and training of young rugby players, it is important to stress such individuals are often the most rewarding to train but also the least understood. Strong evidence suggests strength training young rugby players is both beneficial and safe, and our ability to train key physiological, physical and psychological windows of adaptation will reap rewards later in the athlete's career. As coaches, there is an obligation to train all players in a safe, quality-driven environment that ensures the greatest chance for injury prevention. Knowing the key windows of opportunity to train skeletal growth, the nervous system and the hormonal system is paramount. Young players, just like in their academic pursuits, need to learn and achieve a level of physical literacy that means as they grow and develop their body their nervous system has the correct platform from which to develop.

This group, more than any other, needs a long-term, process-driven training plan. It can be easy for coaches to be sidetracked by success at junior national levels. However, if the sole driver is purely the success of the young player as an individual, then their success will be determined by how they perform as an adult. It is then, and only then, that we will see the payback for an intelligent, process-driven youth training programme.

3 | THE LONG-TERM PHYSICAL DEVELOPMENT OF RUGBY PLAYERS

The long-term physical development of young rugby players is an area that requires significant consideration when delivering strength and conditioning. While youth training is often misunderstood, with many myths associated, it is one of the major 'windows of opportunity' with regards to developing fit, healthy players in later years. Not only are there significant sporting benefits, it should form a significant part of any youngster's physical and social development. Often, while the physical development in areas such as strength, speed and endurance are quite apparent, it is perhaps the social and behavioural benefits that are often less so. Youngsters who partake in a consistent, appropriate programme of physical development tend to exhibit a greater confidence, social awareness and level of communication skills than those who do not. The value of these traits will not only translate into any sporting environment but will also be fundamental to all-round development. We currently have escalating sedentary behaviour in the young and a host of associated health and behavioural issues as a result. Young athletes seem less exposed to the fundamental building blocks of athleticism as free play, and an active lifestyle has become an alien concept in a modern society.

Alongside this, we are experiencing changes in the delivery of physical education in schools and sports clubs. Where once 'time served' teachers delivered a wide-ranging physical education programme to children, we now see a greater emphasis on 'games'. And while these have their place in sporting and athletic development, they become counterproductive when children have not achieved key benchmarks in physical literacy. Just as literacy and numeracy are taught through a developing, progressive rigid framework, so too must physical education. We seem to live in a society that demands success from youngsters in game-related competitions but we have neglected to teach the fundamental building blocks that will allow this. It is the equivalent of asking young people to work out long division without ever having taught the basic skills and knowledge of numeracy. Just as the classroom is vital to academic learning, the playground, sports hall and playing field are vital to athletic development.

The development of young athletes is an area where many sports have sought to put in place a long-term development framework for coaches to work alongside. The young athlete is a unique and challenging proposition to train. However, it is ultimately a rewarding one in that these vital years form the platform for all future sporting development. Young athletes tend to be routinely exposed to high degrees of sports-specific training through games, often with extensive playing schedules (1), yet the same cannot be said for basic physical development. You only need to look at the average competition load of a youngster who is playing both weekly for his school team and often at weekends for a club team. Over the course of a school year and season we will see significant volumes of game time. Crucially, though, they are being exposed to these high competition schedules at a time when they are experiencing a wide range of physical, physiological and psychological changes as a result of their stage of biological maturation (2). As strength and conditioning coaches, we not only need to acknowledge this but also programme in interventions accordingly.

A common question both coaches and parents ask during these formative years is 'is training safe?' If so, at what age and what methods are best? There are certainly correct approaches to training developing athletes and it is also fair to say training incorrectly, no matter what stage of development a player is at, will always have negative effects. Traditionally, rugby has sought to place more emphasis on technical proficiency than physical ability during these years. But as the game has evolved we have taken many long-term training models from other sports. Balyi and Hamilton (3) put forward the widely accepted Long-term Athlete Development Model (LTAD).

They found through the various maturation stages there were acute physical characteristics that should be trained at key windows of opportunity. Although limited in that there are rigid timescales and a lack of empirical evidence, they highlighted that key neural and physiological characteristics should be trained at key phases, e.g. structural development and central nervous system development. This must be aligned with the phases of maturation and the biological development of adolescents. Both this model and the later Youth Physical Development Model (4) require us to understand some key terminology to assist with appropriate programming.

CHRONOLOGICAL AGE

The chronological age is the number of years since birth for an individual. While in essence this seems very straightforward, differing rates of maturation and biological development mean two players can be the same age yet vastly different in stature and appearance. Rugby particularly illustrates this. Across any one school year, we have players who can be separated by eleven months if their birthdays happen to be at the start of the year as opposed to the end. Through puberty this can mean the difference between a boy and a young man in terms of physical development. It is no surprise a team full of September and October birthday players will be physically superior to counterparts born at the end of the school year for the simple reason they are the best part of a year older. Yet they still play in the same year group. In fact, they exhibit a much different physical appearance and skill set to their counterparts.

STAGE OF DEVELOPMENT

Likewise, we have youngsters who are early developers and those who are late. Sadly, there is a tendency in many outcome-driven representative structures to discard the late developer. Ironically, a little more time invested in these developers over time will bear more success. Drop-out rates in early developers tend to escalate far above those of late developers as maturation catches up. It is also true these late developers tend to overtake the group they previously trailed in the specific physical characteristics such as speed and strength. The stages of development can be categorized as pre-puberty, puberty and post-puberty.

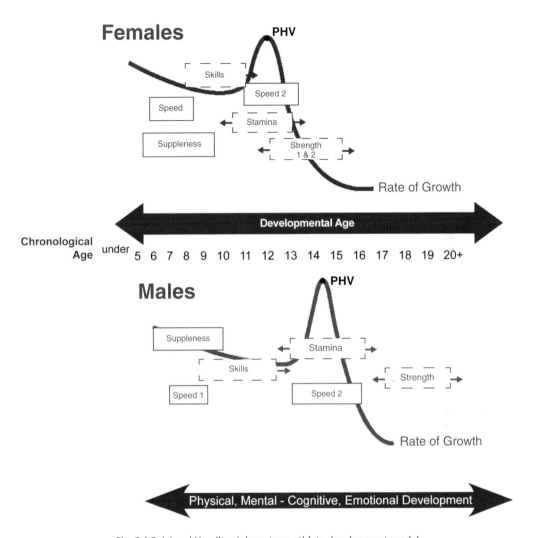

Fig. 3.1 Balyi and Hamilton's long-term athlete development model.

TRAINING AGE

This is the number of years of formalized training experience an individual has, specifically structured, monitored training rather than a global level of activity. Players can be early developers, with a greater chronological age than someone else, yet still have a training age of zero. It is often pretty evident within a group environment when players have a greater training age. They have already started a journey of training

learning and it becomes apparent very quickly. They will look more athletic, display greater levels of athleticism and tend to have the ability to learn and master athletic skills quickly.

Peak Height Velocity: The maximum rate of growth during the adolescent growth spurt.

Peak Weight Velocity: The maximum rate of growth in body weight, generally occurring post PHV.

43

YOUTH PHYSICAL DEVELOPMENT (YPD) MODEL FOR MALES																			
CHRONOLOGICAL AGE (YEARS)	2	3	4	5	6	7	8	9	10	11	12	13	14	15	16	17	18	19	20	33+
AGE PERIOD	EARLY CHILDHOOD		MIDDLE CHILDHOOD								ADOLESCENCE									ADULTHOOD
GROWTH RATE	RAPID GROWTH ←→ STEADY GROWTH ←→ ADOLESCENT SPURT ←→ DECLINE IN GROWTH RATE																			
MATURATIONAL STATUS	YEARS PRE PHV ← PHV → YEARS POST PHV																			
TRAINING ADAPTATION	PREDOMINANTLY NEURAL (AGE-RELATED) ←→ COMBINATION OF NEURAL AND HORMONAL (MATURITY-RELATED)																			
PHYSICAL QUALITIES	FMS		**FMS**		**FMS**		FMS													
	SSS		**SSS**		**SSS**		SSS													
	Mobility		**Mobility**				Mobility													
	Agility		**Agility**				**Agility**						Agility							
	Speed		**Speed**				**Speed**						Speed							
	Power		**Power**				**Power**						Power							
	Strength		**Strength**				**Strength**						Strength							
	Hypertrophy						Hypertrophy		**Hypertrophy**										Hypertrophy	
	Endurance & MC		**Endurance & MC**				**Endurance & MC**						Endurance & MC							
TRAINING STRUCTURE	UNSTRUCTURED		LOW STRUCTURE				MODERATE STRUCTURE				HIGH STRUCTURE				VERY HIGH STRUCTURE					

Fig. 3.2 The youth physical development model.

Fig. 3.2 illustrates the Youth Physical Development Model (4) and highlights the difficulty created by the disparity between chronological age and maturation in young sports people. But, with a more all-round approach, the model looked less at the supposed windows of opportunity and more about all-encompassing programmes. At any one stage, while acknowledging there is a main focus for training, the model suggested we do not abandon all other training. One common criticism of Balyi and Hamilton's LTAD model (3) is that it addressed physiological characteristics in very rigid, 'boxed off' stages. Invariably developing one skill, then abandoning it to concentrate on a further skill meant positive adaptations could be lost. By again keeping all methods of training going but merely loading one a little more at any specific time the hope would be to create a more balanced, all-round athlete who not only has a synergy between both the physical and technical elements but is also able to be adaptable to different sporting challenges and situations. While being proficient in one dimension will yield some success for a period of time, ultimately it will always become predictable and thus easy to read in the long term. Both models look at these key adolescent stages with boys (twelve to sixteen years) and girls (eleven to fifteen years) based around the growth spurt. Certainly, before the 'adolescent growth spurt' training should always focus on motor skill development. There will still be strength adaptations as a result of this but this phase is paramount to ensuring skill acquisition in youngsters.

When the growth spurt does arrive we will see a phase of physical development during which growth hormones and sex hormones such as testosterone are increased significantly (5). In these stages we can see a paradox of impeded performance alongside acute increases in strength and stature. The growth spurt often occurs alongside a period of awkwardness in the young rugby player. Significant growth in anthropometrical terms will require a period of time for technical and movement ability to catch up. Young players experiencing a significant growth spurt may find the body they could control effortlessly six months ago no longer reacts how they want. The elasticity in newly stretched ligaments means a less stable and more inflexible player. It is vital in this stage that both coaches and players are aware of these changes and situations are handled appropriately.

Based on these models, we have a scenario where it is evident that when planning for the overall development of young rugby players we have to place as much emphasis on the physical development as the technical. However, in many sporting clubs and schools we still see a situation where children overplay and undertrain. As a result, they never realize their potential or fail to stay engaged in the game. Young players need a programme of activity that encourages physical competency. This is achieved as a result of players being taught fundamental athletic and movement skills at the same time as fundamental sport skills. This is what is going to give the greatest chance for success in performance, as well as success in participation and general health. It is therefore essential that these interventions are not only put in place but also that players, parents and coaches are educated about the process.

Regardless of whether or not we are chasing achievement in a specific sport or just looking for the social and health-related benefit of rugby, competence and ability in these physical skills will always be the basis for technical skills. If we take a young developing forward as an example, in order to achieve a technically sound and safe scrummaging position he must be stable, supple and strong but most of all, be able to hold an efficient posture, keeping his back flat. So, if he is posturally strong, supple and has a good level of stability we will see the basic technical position can be held. It is only then the player can learn to tactically manipulate techniques in order to become a better player than his competition. The tactical ability and success will be a far-off scenario if the basic physical competency is not there.

So what are the practical applications for using models of LTAD in developing young players? It is certainly the case we need to form a comprehensive but adaptable training, competition and recovery framework if we are to be successful.

Coaching young players while driven by the physiological windows of opportunity must be underpinned by an education process (see Fig. 3.3). Ultimately, we want young players who, whether or not they proceed to levels of higher achievement in the sport or any walk of life for that matter, understand the 'what, when and why' of their training. The more the young player understands the training process, the greater the likely gains. Great coaches are educators and, after the initial learning phase, empower their players to self-direct and understand their training along this training journey.

Fig. 3.3 The process for LTAD in creating adaptable young rugby players.

We must also look to seek and challenge the young player. As a coach, our role is about taking both scientific and coaching principles and applying them to the groups of players we work with. If we want players who can, in time, assess risk and apply the correct tactical strategies we must first expose them to different challenges both on the pitch and in the training room. Youngsters thrive in an environment that has a perfect blend of routine, repetition and refinement, especially in the training of their physical characteristics. We must also not discount the importance of these training environments and the social and behavioural aspect. With increased physical and tactical ability we see increased confidence and discipline. Confident players are always set up to be better players. They are willing to execute skills without hesitation, exactly what we want in game scenarios. Likewise, players with discipline and controlled actions consciously have an impact on results, knowing just when to apply technical and tactical skills. These in turn further foster competitive 'real world' experiences, without which the very foundation of sport would not exist. As a coach, you have to supplement a declining physical education curriculum in schools and increasing sedentary behaviour. It is in the interests of both players and coaches to ensure young players are in the best physical and health-related condition they can be.

Supported with these sound fundamental scientific principles, the planning of youth training must also look to overturn some of the common movement and athletic contra-indications we currently see in young players. While at the elite end of the game a picture is painted of young physical specimens who are coming through to transform the modern game, it is important we do not lose sight of the fact that they are not representative of the groups most of us work with. While there will always be outliers across training groups, it would be prudent to assume catering for the needs of the 'average Joe' players. It is they who will form the majority of your squads.

Such is the importance of an all-encompassing physical literacy, arguably no player should lose sight of these fundamental skills. Fig. 3.4 shows issues a group of developing players would typically present you with.

POOR OVERALL LEVELS OF CONDITIONING

It is not uncommon to find lower levels of conditioning across the board in young players. It is something that should be considered when new training regimes are started. Initially, players will struggle with what may appear straightforward warm-ups and exercise programmes. Ultimately, falling activity levels and what we have come to accept physically in young players means they no longer seem to be able to endure physically challenging and demanding sessions as they could fifteen to twenty years ago. As a result, addressing this imbalance must be the first port of call. All youngsters should be fit enough to train and play.

POOR HIP COMPLEX CONTROL AND STABILITY

The ability to flex and fully extend in the hip complex combined with poor stability and strength mechanics can lead to increases in injury. Commonly, there are high incidences of knee injuries in young players that derive more from dysfunctional hip stability rather than any great acute variables. In order to be athletic, this must be addressed and developed.

PELVIC/LUMBAR INSTABILITY AND TIGHTNESS

The increasingly sedentary lifestyles, battling a 'games console culture' and the fact youngsters tend to be in a seated position for large amounts of the day, leads to tightness

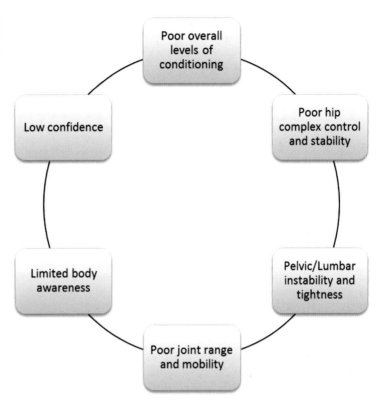

Fig. 3.4 Common physical issues seen in young developing players.

and compromised movement. These mean overall athletic movements are dictated by the players' limitations, rather than external influences. Limited movement in game situations can again lead to potential injury.

POOR JOINT RANGE AND MOBILITY

Growth spurts and not exercising joints through full ranges of motion lead to inefficient joint range. This will lead to over-compensation in other joints and musculature and a poorer set of general movement patterns.

LIMITED BODY AWARENESS

Poor overall kinaesthetic awareness creates challenges when coaching complex movement patterns. It is also a contributing factor for poor technical ability in sport-specific skills. We need to create multi-faceted, multi-dimensional players.

LOW SELF-CONFIDENCE

The effect of low self-confidence cannot be underestimated. Players who lack confidence not only struggle to engage in structured training programmes but also present us with a challenge in terms of creating competitive teams. Also through the years of puberty we are likely to see increased levels of emotional issues are experienced as young players learn to cope with what is a challenging time in their development.

While they are all as a result of overall neglect in training, we can still pinpoint specific physical characteristics to train and target.

47

STRENGTH

Undoubtedly strength training in developing players is an area of great debate and often myth. Once an area deemed dangerous and inappropriate, there is now a substantial body of evidence to support strength training in the young with a range of health and injury prevention benefits (2). With player welfare at the forefront of many current directives, as much as 50 per cent of injuries in youth sport could be avoided with the right strength and conditioning programmes (6, 7). It is in the interests of players, parents and coaches to ensure safety and injury prevention. If players are unfit to train, they will not be fit to play. While injury is part and parcel of playing sport, the ability to reduce the incidence of this and programme specific interventions to prevent it must always underpin the process. Commonly at school level, size plays a significant role in success, often with the larger team having a distinct advantage over their smaller counterparts. We are not all going to have this 'luxury' of more physically advanced players and thus we need to make all players physically capable of holding their own.

Strength increases in adolescence requires a sensible ethical approach with the long-term development of that player in mind. It is in the period before, during and post puberty that we see significant natural strength gains from a number of factors. Strength increases in children and pre-pubescent teenagers appear more to be a result of development in the central nervous system. As they attain a greater intramuscular coordination, we see strength increases but not an increase in size; it is simply a process of their bodies learning skills and becoming more effective and skilled in the mind/body connection. As a result, this phase should see substantial time spent on the fundamental motor skill development. It is exactly this development that will allow young players to excel, especially once the maturation process reaches the significant stage of increased testosterone, growth hormone and so on.

During the adolescent growth spurt, as discussed, young players can become somewhat awkward as their bodies adjust their increased height and weight. While there is a period of catch up, it is still possible to strength-train although the emphasis should be more on a proficiency in handling body weight alongside teaching the technical elements of lifting weights. It would still not be appropriate to load the skeletal system too much through this phase. It is an ideal time for further motor skill and technical skill development. It is often a useful time to teach the technical aspects of weightlifting movements using broomsticks. Patterns such as lunging, squatting, jumping and pressing can be taught with no load, meaning players become technically proficient prior to adding this. These lifts or derivative lifts will form part of the young players' strength/power programme in years to come. They are both highly technical and require significant training of the neural system. Becoming proficient during these years will lead to a far more seamless transition into loaded exercise and will lead to far greater future success in the lifts.

Once players have come through the adolescent growth spurt loaded strength training can begin. I do not think it can be stressed enough that a conscientious professional coach must exhibit some real restraint through this process. In a game where size will always be a significant factor, it can be easy to fall into the trap of loading exercise too early in the hope of building giants. Always remember as a coach it is your job to prepare players to be the best rugby players possible. This does not mean the best at under-14 or -15 level, it means being the best long term. The likelihood for most coaches is that we are merely part of any one player's journey. At some point, if those players are successful we need to hand them on to the next level. It is far better to hand on a good advert of your work rather than one of poor programming and coaching. The correct prescription and delivery of strength work is possibly the greatest injury prevention tool you will have as a coach. As well as enhancing bone development (8), many studies have shown the efficacy in strength training with developing athletes (2, 9). No matter what the age, strength will always fundamentally underpin all athletic qualities. The control of static body weight movement has to be mastered if there is to be any hope of controlling strength in a dynamic situation. For example, if a player is not strong and stable on one leg through full ranges of motion, how can we expect them to change direction effectively at high speed in a game situation?

But what about the practical application of strength training? We have seen across the game that often we do not have access to hi-tech facilities, and training will reflect this. Prior to puberty and Peak Height Velocity (PHV), most resistance training should take the form of technical learning and the control of body weight. There is a great deal of benefit in directing players towards three areas in which to maintain and develop strength and motor skill:

- **Gymnastics:** Sadly, the demise of physical education has certainly been no more evident than in a total decline of gymnastics being taught to youngsters. Although once ever present in most schools, it is now rare to see the basics taught at all. The strength, control and stability it can give youngsters is vital in all ground-based sports and cannot be underestimated.
- **Athletics:** Many youngsters who play rugby over the winter months often do very little extra-curricular sport in the summer months. Athletics gives an opportunity not only to become more technically adept in wider ranging sports but also a crucial opportunity to develop the basic athletic skills of running, jumping and throwing. These are technical tasks that require both concerted practice and good technical coaching. Relatively unloaded, they will not only prepare young players

physically but also neurally. It is no good having big strong players if they cannot operate explosively. Too often we see large lumbering players who seem to have one steady constant speed. There is little variation in pace, with little ability to exert themselves more explosively when called upon. We want players who accelerate when required, change direction explosively and display power in the correct parts of a game.

- **Judo:** Finally, I feel young players can develop considerably through judo. While the similarities in terms of grappling and hip-based explosive movements is evident, it is perhaps the control and cognitive elements where the most benefit is to be found. It teaches youngsters when to apply a lot of force, in big throws, but also when to use the movement and actions of the opponent to their advantage. This multi-faceted skill set will allow for more options as a rugby player. And the more options, the greater the chance of success. Crucially, I think judo (and many other traditional combat sports) offer young players discipline, respect and structure. It is training habits such as this that will form the basis of all future training.

From here, as the players travel through maturation, strength work can begin in earnest. Like all skill acquisition, the emphasis must be on technical mastery and developing players who can move through full ranges of movement with the ability to use the right amount of strength at the right time. With regards to equipment, the challenge of most sparse training environments actually facilitates good quality training. Often, only having access to a few simple pieces of equipment means we need a more streamlined programme of work. As a result, we tend to see better results and a deeper understanding in a few areas, rather than a shallow understanding and proficiency across numerous areas.

Training Experience	Beginner	Intermediate	Experienced	Advanced
Intensity (%1RM)	BW 50-70% of 1RM	60-80% of 1RM	60-80% of 1RM	85-100% of 1RM
Speed of Movement	Moderate-fast	Moderate-fast	Moderate-fast	Maximal
Rest (min)	1	1-2	1-2	2-5
Recovery (hours)	72-48	72-48	72-48	48-24
Sessions Per Week	2-3	2-3	2-3	2-5
Number of Exercises Per Set	6-10	3-6	3-6	2-5
Vol (Sets and Reps)	1-2 of 8-12	2-4 of 6-10	2-4 of 5-8	2-5 of 2-5

Fig. 3.5 Guidelines for training youth athletes. (Adapted from Lloyd, R. S., Faigenbaum, A. D., Myer, G. D., Stone, M. H., Oliver, J. L., Jeffreys, I., Moody, J., Brewer, C., & Pierce, K. (2012). UKSCA position statement: Youth resistance training. *Professional Strength and Conditioning, 26*, 26–39)

We should, however, expose players to a full range of resistance training methods. We have already discussed the need to develop physical competency with body weight, which should always be a 'go to' for players at any age. After that, strength training can be supplemented with use of medicine balls, sand bags, weight discs and bands. Although basic means of creating external resistance, these pieces of equipment are effective and versatile. Relatively cheap to buy, they can be transported easily and mean young players do not need hi-tech gyms. Strength training can be used at the start of a session as a part of a directed warm-up. That way, the players can train and learn together without needing to allocate extra training hours in an already congested week. Fig. 3.5 gives a comprehensive guide for applying practically strength training with young players. In my experience, most of the players we will be working with fall into the beginner and intermediate classifications.

However, the adolescent body is such that,

in pretty short spaces of time, significant gains can be made. One method I have found to be most effective in training these groups is the use of 'complexes'.

Complex training: Adapted from earlier work by Istvan Javorek (10) and Vern Gambetta, complexes represent a time/equipment-friendly method of 'grooving in' fundamental motor and movement patterns using simple equipment. I have found them a practical solution to issues developing players have had with limited access to gyms and equipment. As a concept, they work by layering four similar movement patterns on top of each other and are done consecutively. By doing so, we are able to have a relatively high volume, and thus a muscular endurance component, but done in a short space of time. It is imperative that the movement pattern is coached correctly though, as inadequate technique will only layer bad work on bad.

The use of complexes can be really formed by what individual coaches see as the primary

Complex 1 – Dumbells
(High pull, Snatch high pull, BOR, Squat press)

HIGH PULL

SNATCH HIGH PULL

BOR

SQUAT PRESS

A complex uses exercises done in a continuous order. So here you would do:

6 x High pull
6 x Snatch high pull
6 x BOR
6 x Squat press

That would be one round.

Fig. 3.6 Effective approach to the long-term training of developing rugby players.

Complex 2 – Body weight
(Lunge forward, Diagonal, Lateral)

LUNGE FORWARD

DIAGONAL

LATERAL

A complex uses exercises done in a continuous order. So here you would do:

4 x Forward
4 x Diagonal
4 x Lateral

That would be one round.

On all lunges, the foot of the non-working leg faces forward.

Start with 'raising'. As you get stronger, raise with dumbells.

Fig. 3.6 (continued)

areas for development. This will come from their understanding of the groups they are working with but also their observations in their sessions. The examples in Fig. 3.6 show some simple options that address fundamental areas of development for developing young rugby players.

METABOLIC CONDITIONING AND ENERGY SYSTEM DEVELOPMENT

There has been much debate over whether specific aerobic and anaerobic training should be carried out during the phases of development. The energy systems develop with the hormonal changes during maturation and, because the anaerobic system is not developed fully, there may be some benefit in training it. It is important young developing rugby players are fit for purpose. Commonly, we have seen playing sport through school and club environments as the main opportunity to develop fitness. But this only works if the level of sports specific skills are at a level above habitual. All too often we are seeing a reduced amount of time playing and training in our adolescents. And, crucially, we are seeing an environment that seems happy with creating mediocrity athletically. Young players thrive on a consistent, coordinated approach to physical activity underpinned with regular competition. They have adaptable capable 'engines' and these are still best conditioned through sport-specific skills. However, it is important to create multi-faceted players with regards to energy system development. The benefits of a wide-ranging experience in a broad spectrum of sporting and athletic pursuits is not only evident physically but equally cognitively. The best players come from multi-sport backgrounds where they have been exposed to a multitude of movement strategies and outcomes. With this comes a far more comprehensive understanding of loco-motion, anticipation of play and execution. Thus, when faced with greater challenges in game scenarios, there is a hard-wired physical and mental toolbox that offers options to the player. As a guiding rule, expose young players to as much variation as possible through different types of games and sports.

SPEED, AGILITY AND PLYOMETRIC TRAINING

Discussed in greater depth later, the question of speed training and the use of jump training in the young requires careful consideration with the coach. As with any athlete, it is important to remember speed is partly a genetic quality that, no matter how good the coach, will be hard to manufacture. However, significant gains can still be made on a technical level. Effective coaching of running mechanics should be an integral part of the coach's repertoire with young players. Unloaded, there are reduced concerns over loading incorrectly. Running mechanics and basic sprint training offers a viable method of integrating high velocity training into programmes. As with the lifts and any skill-based task though, the ability to accelerate and run at top speed correctly relies again on coaching the technical model. Poor running mechanics come from poor posture, inability to extend through the hips and joint instability. Integration of some basic drills can improve these qualities radically, alongside the undeniable injury prevention and neural benefits. Likewise, it is important agility and plyometric progressions follow the same coaching process. Eccentric strength and control are fundamental to both these physical characteristics and their development must find its way into players' development.

SUPPLENESS AND STABILITY

Through the adolescent years, young players suffer from somewhat of a paradox with

Neck	Stability – Players should be able to keep the neck stabilized in a neutral position
Shoulder	Stability and mobility – There is a need for the shoulder to be able to move with equal ease, both anteriorly and posteriorly. However, it is also vital stability can be attained at the required time
Thoracic	Mobility – Correct thoracic function is needed to maintain sound postural integrity
Lumbar/hip complex	Stability and mobility – Stable hips are strong hips. Without stability, force will not be able to be directed down through the ground to assist explosive movement
Knee	Stability – Stability at the knee reduces the risk of injury and energy dissipation
Ankle	Mobility – Full ankle mobility will allow efficient movement and reduce injury risk

Fig. 3.7 The relationship between mobility and stability in players.

regards to suppleness and stability. In early stages, we see joint instability occurs and suppleness and flexibility are common. We will have all trained boys and girls who seem to be able to contort to all manner of challenging positions while also looking a little unsteady at times. But, as they move through the adolescent growth spurt, there comes a period of awkwardness. Growth spurts result in changes in the stabilizing ability of tendons and ligaments. Increased body weight and height create challenges with control around the key joint sites. Commonly, we also see a massively reduced mobility around the joints as a result of more sedentary lifestyles over these challenging teenage years and overall muscular imbalance.

Issues with mobility and stability can again be reduced with players who have taken part in prior gymnastic activity and have fundamental control benefits from athletic training.

Further to this, any programme that focuses on large compound movements through a full range of motion, and one that looks to train all fundamental movement qualities equally, will deliver stable, mobile and strong players. Fig. 3.7 shows how there must be interplay between stability and mobility for all-round athletic ability. If any of these areas create a weak link, the chain of movement in the body will break down.

While training and developing young players is a challenge, it is perhaps one of the most rewarding groups and an area that is growing significantly within the UK. When done correctly, the results in future success both on and off the pitch cannot be underestimated. That being said, it is an area that needs strong, educated coaches who not only have the underpinning scientific knowledge but also the coaching and communication style to develop young players/athletes.

4 PERFORMANCE TESTING FOR RUGBY UNION

Performance testing for the strength and conditioning coach is fundamental to the whole athletic development process. Done correctly, it gives an opportunity for planning but also the crucial reflection process. This will allow us to see if training interventions have worked and also give us valuable data in player evaluations that will not only assist their development but also help coaches in team selection.

The golden rule for testing, though, must be that if we are to collect data on players it has to inform and direct our practice. There is no benefit in merely testing players if it does not change what we do. Testing is labour intensive, both in carrying out the testing and in the analysis of results, so a more streamlined approach may serve you better. There should be an element of caution with all testing, however, and a realization the test is merely a picture of that moment in time. While it will give us information, this information may not always be absolute. Factors such as fatigue, time of year, injury, hydration and so on can alter results and as coaches we should look at test results in conjunction with many other variables.

So what makes an effective performance test?

Specificity: First and foremost, the test has to be specific. In simple terms: does it actually tell us what we need to know? Test selection should be guided by physiological and biomechanical parameters. If we are testing maximal strength or speed, for example, then we need a test that does exactly that. The test must look to measure only one variable, with no interference from other factors.

Accuracy: Tests must be repeatable and ultimately accurate. Using the same repeated conditions for re-tests and accurate equipment will ensure results can be compared. If tests are carried out on different surfaces, for example, it must be noted. Conducting a test on a field in summer will give differing results to those carried out in winter. Likewise, weather changes and timings may have an effect.

Validity: There are standardized tests that hold up under scientific analysis and these are generally the reliable ones we use. There is usually normative data to support most tests, although you may struggle with sub-elite populations. What is important is that your test results are used relative to where you want your players to be and within the group that you test.

Asking a developing adolescent player to equal an adult's athletic standards is unrealistic and inappropriate. Likewise, asking amateur players who train once or twice a week to be similar athletes to professional players is also not going to be an effective comparison. For your own personal use, there is nothing particularly wrong with devising your own test as long as it holds up to reliability validity.

Education: Both coaches and players need to be aware of why tests are being done and how they can relate to the team goals. Players can become despondent quickly if they feel a process is not being done for a valid reason, so coaches must have a period of education. A player who does not see the importance of a test result will seldom give a maximal measure.

Reporting results: A coach must agree before-hand how results are to be reported back to players. Generally, an open sharing of results in team sport is important but sometimes those in younger age groups, women and sensitive players may not feel comfortable having their results shared. Whatever course of action is agreed, that is what should be carried through. A useful process could be:

- Players are informed of test dates, what is being tested and why. It is also a good time to highlight what the end goal is and how increased performance is measured
- Players are tested and results are fed back in a way that the players can understand, engage and react
- Training interventions are programmed
- Training interventions applied
- There is a re-test and feedback of results
- Reflection on areas that can be changed/improved.

Timing: Timing of tests is often a bone of contention with players and coaches over when we can get the best picture of what is going on in the squad. Coaches can sometimes want a

high volume of testing. However, it takes time for an intervention (increased speed work for example) to take effect and testing with too high a frequency will often lead to results that report little change. Although some tests can be carried out more regularly, I think the following is a good timeline for all players' testing schedules:

- Start of pre-season
- End of pre-season
- Pre-Christmas
- Post-Christmas
- End of the season.

Test Selection: There are many test choices for a strength and conditioning coach; these can be guided by the population you are working with, and often by the constraints within which you work. There will always be a 'gold standard', as it were, but sometimes this is just not an option. The key thing is that you are actually testing.

Equipment: Many tests can be done with quite simple equipment but the better the equipment, the more reliable and accurate it will be. As a guide, the following should be useful:

- Cones
- Recording sheets
- Tape measures of varying length
- Stopwatch
- Heart rate monitors
- A jump mat/timing mat
- Electronic speed gates
- A speaker system capable of outdoor use
- Any relevant audio recordings of test protocols (beep test, yo-yo test, etc.).

Test Selection: Fig. 4.1 shows the standard testing battery appropriate for the three case study groups. With regards to the young developing players and the amateur players, it is not necessary to include anaerobic specific tests unless a coach particularly wants to do so.

Test Characteristic	Young Developing Player	Amateur Player	Aspiring Professional Player
Aerobic Tests	Multi-stage fitness test (Beep) YoYo endurance test 2km row Cooper 12min run	Multi-stage fitness test (Beep) YoYo endurance test 2km row Cooper 12min run	Multi-stage fitness test (Beep) YoYo endurance test 2km row Cooper 12min run
Anaerobic Tests	Not necessary	Not necessary	Phosphate recovery test Running bases Anaerobic sprint test (RAST) Wingate testing
Strength Tests	Max press-up test Max inverted row Max BW squat Max chin-up test	Max press-up test Max inverted row Max BW squat Max chin-up test	5, 3, 1 repetition strength testing. Look to test back squat, deadlift, bench press and loaded chin-ups
Power Tests	Vertical jump Broad jump CMJ	Vertical jump Broad jump CMJ	Vertical jump broad jump CMJ 'Reactive strength' tests Med ball throw tests 'Repeated jumps' testing
Speed Tests	Not necessary	Not necessary	'Gate timed' 10m, 20m, 30m, 40m

Fig. 4.1 Example testing battery for young developing players, amateur players and aspiring young professionals.

Owing to the overall importance of the aerobic system and the relatively low level of training age of those playing groups, a measure of their aerobic capacity will be sufficient. Likewise, speed testing is also not really needed. The various jump tests will give us a measure of explosive ability and, therefore, the better these scores are the more likely we will be to have fast powerful players.

These tests are designed to give a picture of players' physical capabilities but can and should be added to as they mature through the training process and reach higher levels of performance. Over time, testing becomes a more integrated approach with physiotherapy staff and strength and conditioning staff working together with biomechanical and movement screening. These tests look at players' structure and movement and highlight areas of tightness/weakness and instability, all of which could compromise athletic function.

Players at the elite end of the game will also carry out daily monitoring around physical and mental readiness, fatigue and preparedness for training/performance. The more elite the player, the more that rides on performance and getting the most out of players is paramount. It is a fine balance between volume and intensity of training that can have both positive and negative adaptation.

5 | TRAINING STRENGTH AND POWER IN RUGBY UNION

Both strength and power are fundamental physical characteristics that need to be trained in rugby players. Locomotive activities such as running, jumping, sprinting and stopping are skills that highlight a player's ability to express power, and power can only occur on the back of a solid foundation of strength. The greater those maximal strength levels, the greater the opportunity for players to produce maximal power (1, 2, 3). Added to this, many positional sport-specific skills such as grappling, tackling, scrummaging, mauling and so on will require a player to be able to call on reserves of strength and power.

Historically, rugby has always flirted with manipulating resistance training to produce bigger, stronger and faster players, although it has to be said at times the underpinning scientific rationale has been lost in translation. We have seen a transition both in methods of training and the physical appearance of players as a result. While in the past players spent a large amount of their training time on getting as 'fit' as possible, the modern player spends a greater amount of time looking to change the size structure and physiological ability of his or her body through training with resistance. We have also seen a greater acceptance and understanding that stronger, more robust, players are more resistant to injury. As much as a third of injuries have been reported to be reduced as a result of consistent resistance training, with 50 per cent of over-use injuries halved by strength training (Laurenson et al., 2014 bjsm [4]). But, as with all training, we must first fully understand what exactly strength and power are before we can look to elicit adaptations through differing training methods.

Even finding a general consensus on what is resistance training and what methods are best placed to produce a multi-dimensional, multi-faceted, strong and powerful player is hard. The modern player not only needs robustness through a number of positions but also the ability to coordinate a wide array of movement choices and, crucially, do so with appropriate levels of resistance.

But what methods are best? Are some better than others? Through resistance training we know we will have changes and increased size and function of both neural and structural actions (Fig. 5.1). However, choosing the mode of training and the load will guide the adaptations we see. When we train with differing loads and velocities, the load we select exerts forces on the body. We use muscles to either stabilize and resist the load or move the load, thus exerting strength (4). There has

Morphological Changes Affecting Strength and Power	Neural Changes Affecting Strength and Power
We can see changes in muscle fibre type, specifically a hypertrophy of fibres	Increased motor unit recruitment
Changes in the cross sectional area of muscle contributing to greater ability to produce force	Increased firing frequency (Rate coding)
Changes in the architecture of the muscle (i.e. angles of pennation)	A greater ability of intramuscular coordination
Increased tendon strength and stability properties within the MTU	

Figure 5.1 The neural and morphological changes of strength and power training.

Fig. 5.2 Different resistance training terminology.

Resistance Training: Any training modality that involves the use of external resistance. Traditionally this may be a weight, machine or object (barbell, sandbag, medicine ball etc).

Bodyweight Training: Training using the body as the source of resistance. While this may be BW exercise such as press ups, pull ups, it also includes gymnastic movements, wrestling/grappling and suspension training.

Fixed Resistance Machines: Common in healthclubs/public gyms, these generic fixed machines allow users to select loads through a pin selection to increase in weighted increments. They are a relatively user-friendly, safe method of strength training, although have significant drawbacks over free weights training.

Weightlifting: Weightlifting generally refers to exercising with barbells and weight plates. The movements are based around the Olympic Lifts of the Snatch, Clean and the Jerk. It also would cover derivatives of these lifts (RDL, Hang Clean, Push Press etc).

Power-lifting: Involves the training and competing for 1RM maximums in three competition lifts: The Bench Press, Deadlift and Squat.

Explosive/Elastic Power Training: Explosive training can describe ballistic and accelerative training such as concentric only work, prowler pushing and acceleration. Elastic power training requires utilization of the Stretch Shortening Cycle, best seen in Plyometric Training.

been much debate over the years as to the best way to train strength and power to be most effective in these sporting situations. There is often confusion over how one type of training differs from another and it is worth understanding some of the styles and the potential adaptations.

It is important to train this full range of modalities if we want a truly multi-dimensional rugby player. Underneath, all strength-ability players will be dictated to a degree by their levels of genetic strength. Put simply, some individuals are naturally stronger than others. In part, some of this is born into individuals but

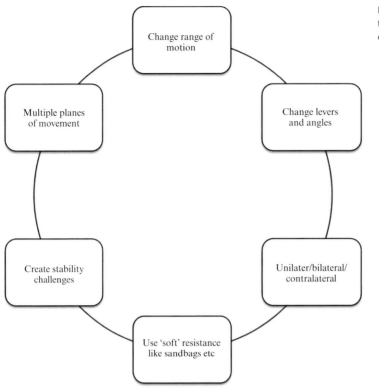

Fig. 5.3 Different ways that body weight can be challenged.

it is the early years where we can nurture it. Falling activity rates in youngsters, as already mentioned, have presented challenges in that we see fewer functionally strong individuals. Gymnastics, wrestling, climbing and so on provide a great foundation for young players. To be able to control and direct our own movement through a full range of body weight movement and activities at a young age 'bullet-proofs' the body from injury and creates a solid, robust structural framework. We want to create a connection between both the muscles and the mind, where we have well-trained neural pathways. We should always master body weight training before we look to load exercises. Sadly, it is an area players and coaches commonly wish to speed through, resulting in the long term in reduced capacity to develop. Fig. 5.3 shows some of the ways body weight can still be challenged and developed.

Bodybuilding methods, that is training in a manner whereby we see a development and hypertrophy of the musculature, again presents us with an opportunity not only for an increase in stature but, crucially, it allows us to develop areas of muscle in the body to aid protection in what is a physical contact sport. However, the key is that we work on functional hypertrophy as opposed to aesthetically driven programmes. The bodybuilding community is time-served in strategies to increase lean muscle, albeit to be visually impressive as opposed to functionally effective. As a coach, it is your task to use the methods appropriately to aid further development. We must still be driven by the goal of whether the gains we are making ultimately make us better players. That is what functional hypertrophy is – its results aid our function in rugby.

From there we can increase strength and

maximal strength significantly, with many training regimes taken from powerlifting. There is merit in the long-term programming of maximal strength development through these core lifts. For example, if an athlete can squat double their body weight they will have a greater ability to express power vertically and horizontally over weaker counterparts. As already stated, these movements that put athletes through both flexion and extension at the ankle knee and hip are key determinants of athletic ability (5).

Once we have built a solid foundation in strength we can look to develop our explosive capability. Athletic success is determined by the ability to not only produce these high levels of strength but, vitally, being able to produce these high rates of force in as short a time as possible (4). Sprinting, jumping and changes of direction require an explosive capability and are highly correlated with being strong (1, 2, 6). Power training, as a result, needs to be programmed to stimulate the synthesis of the contractile proteins, increase filament muscle density and create more efficient neural pathways. The most efficient way to achieve this is to train both with Olympic weightlifting movements and their derivatives, explosive training-like jumps, medicine ball throws, sprints and acceleration and plyometric training. We are required to load players and develop them to express high rates of force in short timescales through flexion and extension at the ankle, knee and hip joints. This movement mimics all athletic movements of sprinting, jumping, cutting direction and so on. As a result of this training method, we get adaptions that assist the explosive capability of players:

- Players learn to be as explosive as possible but in the shortest possible time with maximal intent
- Players develop high rates of force production, meaning not only can they produce a high level but they can call on it quickly
- This results in players having increased recruitment of the fast twitch fibres and,

crucially, the frequency at which they are recruited (rate coding)

- There is significant hypertrophy, or an increase in size, of these important fast twitch fibres
- The mind muscle synchronization is developed through more efficient motor programmes. Being explosive, and training to do so, habitually requires significant time investment and should be seen as a skill similar to sport-specific skill
- Finally, the player will develop a greater capacity to do explosive work and, with the intermittent nature of rugby, this makes him or her more likely to produce high rates of force later in the game, generally when games are won and lost.

STRENGTH (FORCE PRODUCTION)

Strength = the ability to produce force (in both magnitude and direction) against external resistance (7).

Better rugby players tend to be stronger and, thus, are able to apply more force at critical moments in game situations. It goes without saying the more we are able to train someone in the maximal production of force, the more potential for athletic success they will have. Athletic movements and success over opponents are positively correlated to many athletic performance variables (8, 9) when strength levels are increased. While historically one of the myths of strength training was it made players slow as we associated strength with big powerlifters or strength athletes, the opposite is in fact true. Strength will always be the platform upon which power/explosive activity is based. Maximum levels of strength, that is a player's one repetition maximum, are highly correlated to explosive power events (10), specifically sprinting, jumping and change of direction, and thus have efficacy in being part of a player's overall programming.

It is arguable if players can ever be too strong, however there is consideration needed in the type of strength characteristics players have available.

Strength, like any other quality, will only ever be beneficial if it can be called upon appropriately at the right times. When a player gets to a strength level where the cost of chasing further increased strength outweighs the benefits, then they are likely to be strong enough. This is a prevalent issue as strength training has become more attractive in rugby players. While we know strength plays a vital part as a foundation to power, we often see players chasing absolute strength gains to a point where other characteristics suffer. While absolute strength is important, it is perhaps more realistic to look at development of relative strength as a performance goal. Stronger, more powerful, players relative to their body weight will represent a more efficient player. In part, it may be that measuring strength is straightforward and we can see increases easily. Also, within rugby, as with any other contact sport, there is often a social bravado issue whereby the strongest player is somehow deemed higher on the social ladder. Sadly, the same cannot always be said for athleticism. Players need a varied and well-developed skill set throughout the full spectrum of the force-velocity curve (Fig. 5.4).

There is an inverse relationship to force and velocity and we must train all parts of the curve. Exposing players to training that develops the whole curve will give a deeper strength skill set, and one that will contribute to playing success. Fig. 5.4 shows the relationship between force and velocity when selecting exercises. All training will fall somewhere along this curve and it is vital a coach marries the event demands for players with correct exercise selection. Remember the goal of training will always follow an athlete, sport, position, rationale. We train players as all-round athletes who are strong, fast, powerful, reactive, supple and fit. Only then do we look to increase

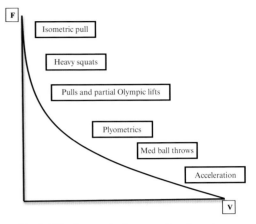

Fig. 5.4 The force-velocity curve showing where different exercise selections sit.

specificity in relation to the sport, and then finally we look at specificity of programming for the position.

If we look at the exercises, we can see they sit along the whole curve. Where you load a player's training will dictate his or her athletic capabilities as a result. There must be an element of the higher force/low velocity training to give *general strength* qualities. Then we have *transitional* strength, allowing a greater speed velocity element and rate of force production. Finally, we will train *specific strength* qualities. These low force/high velocity movements look to have the greatest dynamic correspondence to the game demands but are the icing on the cake, as it were. They are only possible following comprehensive training of the general and transitional strength characteristics.

Fig. 5.5 shows a number of exercises throughout the full curve, covering general, transitional and specific.

- **Isometric pull:** Often used to assess maximal force production, this represents the highest force end of the spectrum. The bar is unable to move, so there is no velocity. As a result, an athlete can impart a maximal level of force production in

General Exercises	Transitional Exercises	Specific Exercises
Compound lifts such as squat/deadlift	Loaded ballistic exercises such as squat jump	Olympic lifts (with athletes of appropriate ability)
Single leg strength	Derivatives such as pulls and shrugs	Plyometrics
Pressing exercises	Trap bar jumps. Concentric only jumps	Agility drills
Pulling exercises	Acceleration	Top speed running

Fig. 5.5 General, transitional and specific strength training exercises.

this position. As discussed, though, there is a time dependency when it comes to success on the rugby field. We have to be quicker to react, quicker to move and more powerful than our opposition while we are doing so. If a player spent too much time training close to this end of the spectrum, while they could produce high levels of force, they would not be able to do it very quickly. It is not uncommon to find players who are heralded as being exceptionally strong, however their strength does not seem to translate on to the field. As previously discussed, what we train for is what we get. At some point, if we only ever train players in slow maximal contractions, we will get players who cannot use the strength they have quickly enough

- **Heavy squats:** As more velocity occurs through the movement we will find exercises such as squatting and deadlifting so long as the load is prescribed to such a level near maximal contraction. It is interesting to note, however, in untrained players with regards to strength training, simple programming of strength with multi-joint, compound lifts will still make players significantly faster and more powerful. Remember, general strength work should always be a mainstay of any programme. Regardless of the rugby specific

event, strength attainment and maintenance will always figure in athletes' programmes. Strong athletes are powerful athletes.

- **Pulls and partial Olympic lifts:** Derivative parts of the Olympic lifts such as shrugs, pulls and partial movements allow players to train explosive capabilities while still being able to use high loads. Due to the time dependency and the fact they are done with maximal intent mean levels of force, production can be increased but also the rate at which we are now producing force.
- **Plyometrics:** Plyometric activity such as jumping, hopping and bounding requires moderate levels of force production to overcome body weight and gravity but at increasingly high velocities to use the stretch reflex of our musculotendinous structures.
- **Med ball throws:** In exercises such as explosive med ball throws, the amount of force required is as a direct result of the weight of the ball. In a movement such as an overhead throw, the relatively low weight of the med ball means significant velocities are used to throw the ball explosively upwards.
- **Acceleration:** Finally, we have acceleration. Significant velocities are needed horizontally but after overcoming the initial

inertia of the body, the levels of force production are pretty low.

As coaches, then, it is imperative we analyse both the strength needs of the sport and then of the individual. Different positional demands in rugby mean players will require differing levels of force and velocity producing capabilities. A front five forward may need greater levels of maximal force production for set piece work, such as scrums, while backs will almost certainly find their needs around the higher velocities lower force end. However, it should be remembered all positions will be required to draw from elements throughout the full force-velocity curve and, thus, no element can afford to be left out of the strength programme.

While we understand that strength, through its relationship with velocity, can take many forms, it is maybe a little more straightforward to look at the concise terms that allow us to understand fully the role differing strength characteristics play in building the complete rugby player. There are distinct differences across the force-velocity relationship between weak and strong individuals (11) and in order

to increase all of these, strength must trained and programmed across the full spectrum of characteristics.

Maximal strength training: This requires rugby players to overcome greater external resistance. The speed of movement will be increased to create a maximum effort. In the gym scenario, it is easy for us to find examples of maximum strength, notably in low rep and single rep maximal lifts. While there are fewer instances in a rugby game to call upon, the increase in maximum strength not only acts as a platform for the production of power (strength at speed) but higher maximum levels of strength will always produce higher sub-maximal levels of strength, which are more common in a game scenario. Maximum strength will always be vital in the production of maximum power with strong rugby players having an increased ability to produce power (9).

Explosive Strength Training: Also called power training, this is undertaken once there is a higher contribution through velocity, specifically acceleration either of the body or an external resistance. If we think of a game of rugby, it is almost entirely comprised of repeated bouts of explosive activity no matter what position a player plays in. By replicating the force-velocity characteristics of these movements and their biomechanical specificity we can make sure we train to achieve the vital dynamic correspondence. It is the difference between our training affecting the outcome on the pitch or merely being a lot of wasted time and energy with little performance gain.

Repeated Strength/Explosive Training: This is the ability not just to carry out explosive movements in a game scenario but, vitally, to have the ability to do so successively. Often termed power endurance, the term is somewhat of a paradox in that the two characteristics, power and endurance, can neither

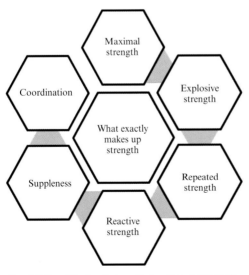

Fig. 5.6 The differing factors that make up strength.

operate together nor are they conducive to each other's success. We are looking to create players who are more explosive but have the capacity to repeat those levels of explosive activity through the game. Often referred to as 'strength-speed', it is this explosive skill set we are seeing more and more in the modern game. As players increase in size and speed, we must also increase our ability to combat this in the contact area.

Reactive Strength Training: Also called plyometric training, this is the other side of the explosive training spectrum, needed to make sure players have that reactive ability to beat the opposition. We see a requirement for a significant speed of movement to overcome a relatively small level of resistance, such as a player cutting to change direction when attacking. The player has to reactively impart force into the pitch, resulting in an explosive change of direction. Often poorly coached and programmed, both maximal strength and explosive strength are fundamental to the development of plyometric and reactive ability. As a result, it will always form part of a long-term approach to developing rugby athletes and should not be seen as an easily achievable strength quality. Not only will it require significant strength and stability levels, it also requires high levels of both intramuscular coordination and a competent use of the neural system.

Suppleness: This can be best described as having flexibility, strength and, importantly, control through the full ranges of motion. While flexibility and stability can play off against each other in the extremes, the ability to control the body consciously, rather than movement being dictated to by the body's limitations, will always mean players are in full control of their movement. This not only gives a greater aptitude for positional sport specific skills, it allows player greater choices in the game scenario. Players are able to execute a greater range in their movement choices and thus will always have a greater set of options in front of them over an opposition player with limitations.

Coordination: This, finally, should link all these other qualities together. Training should look to create a synergy between both the body and the mind, both through quality movement and through efficient neural pathways.

But why then is it so important to look to increase the explosive capabilities of players? We know strength is fundamental to this but the positive outcomes in a sporting arena come not by how much force we can produce but at what rate it can be produced. Mechanical power, the rate at which a player can call upon their strength (5), and overall strength are derived from a number of areas. It is these areas that contribute to create the muscle contraction:

- **Motor neuron impulse:** In order for contraction to occur, we need the signals to be relayed effectively and quickly by the motor neuron, as discussed in Chapter 1.
- **Hypertrophy:** In its basic sense, hypertrophy is the increase of lean muscle mass. Training leads to a breakdown in muscle protein. Resistance training causes repeated increased tension, causing myofibrillar damage (11). With nutritional intervention and recovery, protein synthesis occurs and, as a result, an anabolic growth in lean muscle mass. Hypertrophy in rugby is required for morphological adaptations resulting in an increased ability to produce force/rate of force production and also to increase lean body mass, aiding protection in what is a contact sport.
- **General all-round strength levels:** As with the law of individual differences across any age group, positional group or squad, there will be vastly differing levels of genetic strength. From a genetic standpoint, some people are simply stronger.

Some, as a result of what they have done athletically in their early years' development, can also exhibit differing strength and consequently power levels.

KNOWING THE RESISTANCE TRAINING ENVIRONMENT

While we may have challenges in terms of access to a private facility, it is becoming more and more common for most gyms to have appropriate free weights equipment. While there are a number of benefits to free weights, especially as we look to whole body compound lifts and explosive work, there will still be occasions when gyms simply have mostly fixed resistance machines. They are safe, easy to use and minimum risk, so there are many facilities still like them. One thing worth noting is, although they are second best to free weight equipment, if it is a choice between using them or not training then obviously the former is the sensible choice. Sometimes we have to think outside the box a little with session planning but ultimately if we understand the fundamental principles and variables of training then we should still be able plan a satisfactory session in the short term.

The modern training environment should contain:

- **Lifting platforms:** Generally constructed from rubber and wood, they provide both a safe footing but also an area that weights can be dropped if necessary. In effect, they also mark out a 'work' area, so minimize the risk of collisions.
- **Olympic barbells:** These are designed with bearings and rotating collars. Thus, when the Olympic lifts and their derivatives are performed, the plates rotate allowing for a smooth movement. Standard Olympic barbells are 20kg, although there are also 15kg bars and 10kg training technique bars. Prices range considerably with a competition standard bar costing between £100 and £2,000.
- **Olympic bumper plates:** These are colour/weight coordinated with 25kg (red), 20kg (blue), 15kg (yellow) and 10kg (green). Smaller increments tend to range in colours but the main weights are consistent across the majority of gyms. The bumper plate serves the purpose of setting the bar at a correct height when lifting from the floor but more so that when a bar is dropped in a lift, or in cases of a failed lift, the bumpers do not damage the platform. Metal weights should not be dropped on the platform.
- **Safety clips:** Safety spring collars are used to keep the bumper plates secure.
- **Power racks:** Racks of differing types have the main purpose of a safe structure to lift weight from, and have depth pins that can assist when lifters are not using a spotter.
- **Ancillary equipment:** Further to the equipment above, gyms will also have numerous fixed machines, cardio machines and smaller equipment such as dumb-bells, medicine balls and so on.

It is always wise to gauge the environment you are in. Private health clubs and local authority facilities tend not to allow the dropping of weights or throwing of medicine balls.

STRUCTURING A SESSION

Getting the right structure to exercise selection is vital if you are to benefit from potentiated effects of previous exercises and use the neural and structural adaptions in the correct order. Remember, our session structure will always contain specific exercises. They will be movement specific, physiologically specific and should be related directly to the athletic outcome. While all these elements do not need to be present in all sessions (the focus of the training phase will dictate the content), it is important they follow the order below:

Sample Session A	Sample Session B
Deceleration and landing mechanic drills	Deceleration and landing mechanic drills
Drop jumps 3 × 5	T-Agility drill 3 × 4 each
Power clean 3 × 5	Acceleration starts 3 × 5
Back squat 3 × 5	Hang snatch 3 × 5
Push press 3 × 5	Romanian deadlift 3 × 5
Pull-up 3 × 8	Overhead squat 3 × 5

Figure 5.7 Example session orders.

Recovery Time Between Sets	Recovery Level
0-30sec	~ 50% metabolic recovery
30sec-2min	~90% metabolic recovery
2-3min	Near complete metabolic recovery
3-5min	Near complete neural recovery
5-10min	Complete neural recovery

Figure 5.8 Guideline set recovery times.

- Technical and mobility work
- Neurally driven work
- Explosive/RFD (rate of force development) lifts
- Large compound multi-joint lifts
- Assistance/ancilliary.

Technically challenging work and exercise that has a large neural element from the central nervous system must be done at the start to counteract the effects of only working submaximally if fatigued. Speed is a neural skill. Under fatigue we see a reduction in strength, RFD, power output and technique. So why should we not ask players to try to improve speed or explosiveness with all these elements compromised? Instead of training players to be fast or explosive, we will actually have the opposite effect – they will become slower. What in fact is

happening is we are training a player's capacity to operate submaximally.

Once this work has been done in a session we can load the large, multi-joint compound exercises, followed by the smaller supplementary or assistance exercises. Fig. 5.7 shows two sample session orders that will work with players, assuming they are fully warmed up and have done any pre-habiliative work they have been set.

Recovery Time: Fig. 5.8 shows guideline recovery times for training. It is a fine balance with recovery during a session. We need to look for optimum recovery of the metabolic and neural systems in order that subsequent work sets are performed both at the required level and, more importantly, performed with the body returned to a near optimum state. Remember though, both the volume and intensity, and also exercise selection, will need to be taken into consideration. It can be a difficult process to manage as we tend not to have unlimited time to recover in sessions, often being constrained by large squad numbers or limitations of the training facility that we are in. The best rule of thumb will, of course, always be that you cut your cloth accordingly and work as best you can within the constraints of your environment.

APPLICATIONS FOR STRENGTH AND POWER TRAINING

While some practical applications of strength training are given in the chapter on long-term athlete development, we can discuss a little further the intricacies of this challenging group. Likewise, it is probably sensible to include both the young developing player and the amateur weekend player in the same vein and class them as both relatively weak and untrained. As a result, we have to understand that, in the relatively weak, by simply increasing strength levels we will immediately see an increase in peak power. So the stronger we can get these groups through simple well-programmed exercise interventions the better. It is an important point as often these two groups perceive in order to become faster and more powerful they have to replicate more advanced programmes from elite-trained athletes. As a result, what we often find is players darting from one programme to the next based on what they read, hear or are told is most effective, rather than taking a long-term consistent approach to training. Players must earn the right to progress to the transitional and specific forms of training and that right has to come built on a solid strength foundation. No matter who the player, we must be able to say that to progress they must have the core functions of controlling loads in single/double leg movements, pushing, pulling and resisting force in braced positions. Added to this, they must also be able to both produce force (doing something explosive) and equally reducing force (slowing down).

Once players are time served and have built both a training history and a strength competency, such as aspiring professional players in academy structures, we have to develop our strategy. We are likely to have built a reservoir of strength we need to programme interventions that will allow us to both maintain these levels and develop the ability to produce this force (RFD) in far quicker time frames. Remember, if we have two players of equal strength, the likelihood is the one who will be better in any sporting situation is the one who has the ability to call on that strength quicker. And, similarly, our training should look to elicit this production of force in faster time frames. We need to look to programme a mixed methods approach that not only allows time to maintain, develop and peak max strength but uses a variety of methods to develop the whole characteristics of the force-velocity curve. Training concurrently in this manner better attenuates the gains in players' muscle mass, strength and power as opposed to them simply training strength alone. We will be able to optimize the power generation of our athletes and increase the transfer as the player becomes more rounded and skilled physiologically (12).

As previously stated, it is the mark of a good coach that he or she can apply the biomechanical and physiological rationale in order to get the maximum transfer of training. Players have limited time to train, so the more return we can get on the training investment the better. By combining characteristics across the whole curve, such as heavy resistance training, ballistic training and plyometric activity, we can increase overall RFD and peak power, key determinants of success (5). It is vital never to lose sight of the role integrating dynamic explosive work has in regards to athleticism. It is all too easy, especially in the modern game, to be sidetracked into an obsession with players being the strongest in the squad or league. While important, with trained individuals it is only half the story.

Remember though, as intensity increases so too does a greater need for recovery. While higher volumes can occur in developing athletes who are working to a degree at an accumulation of gross athletic skill, recovery becomes a vital component with trained athletes. It is simply not the case that the more advanced a player gets in training, the more they can endure. They are training at a far higher threshold and thus need the recovery time to allow adaptation.

Consider training as a continuum where a player takes a journey from the novice, who has never trained, to the advanced athlete who displays high levels of aptitude and application in the full range of athletic skills. The journey for about 80 per cent of that continuum is simply the process of consistent, well-planned training. Simple, effective, progressive exercise will reap the physical rewards and, while recovery is important to combat fatigue, the levels at which the players are operating are still at a relatively low threshold, yet with marked gains. However, once we have trained athletes, for the final 20 per cent of the journey we have to work that little bit more intelligently, looking to elicit the smallest marginal gains from well-programmed specific training interventions. It takes a lot more effort to get even the smallest improvement. However, at this level, the success of the individual will often come down to the tiniest of margins.

Because of these training thresholds and the methods used, recovery and time best spent using various methods to recover optimally become a vital focus. The damage and fatiguing adaptions of training are a part of training and physical development but must be acted on to see improvements. Fig. 5.9 shows various recovery windows from different types of training. It is worth noting though that these are guidelines. In untrained players

there is a certain safety blanket if mistakes in programming the training week are made, for the simple fact the level of competition is lower. However, in more elite players we cannot afford to have players take the field in anything other than peak conditioning. While it happens, and is part of the reality of sport, the best teams manage their players to avoid mistakes. As a result, the recovery windows mean the training week must be structured to give optimum recovery time neurally, metabolically and psychologically.

As an underpinning goal, however, there should be a background rationale that sees all players, regardless of ability or level, attaining:

- **Get fit:** All players should, generally speaking, be aerobically fit with an all-round aptitude to do a wide range of work and be able to do it for a prolonged time. It is still very prevalent across all levels of the game that players are no longer as fit as they were. Before we even consider the performance end of the scale, this must always be the starting point. For many junior teams, simply getting more of their squad of players fitter than the opposition will bring results on the pitch.
- **Get strong:** Strength and the ability to control both body weight and external load are required, not only for injury prevention, but to act as the foundation of all other force-velocity relationships. Strength is simple and global at the outset, later developing with more intensity, volume and complexity.
- **Get explosive:** Being explosive and the ability to do this repeatedly throughout a game will form a solid cornerstone of training programmes. Whether through acceleration, the contact situation or set piece, there is a fundamental requirement for all players to not only express force but importantly they must do this with a maximal intent. Often we discuss why some players appear more explosive than

Max strength	• 1–6 sets of 1–3 reps • Load 75–100% 1RM • Recovery 3–5 mins
Max power	• 1–6 sets of 1–3 reps • Load 50–85% 1RM • Recovery 3–>5 mins
Strength development	• 1–6 sets of 3–6 reps • Load 75–100% 1RM • Recovery 3–5 mins
Power development	• 1–6 sets of 3–6 reps • Load 50–85% 1RM • Recovery 3–5 mins
Functional hypertrophy	• 1–10 sets of 6–10 reps • Load 60–90% 1RM • Recovery 30s–2 mins
Muscular endurance	• 8+ sets > 1–3 reps • Load 40–70% 1RM • Recovery 0–30s

Fig. 5.9 Sets, reps, loading and recovery for strength and power training.

others and, while it occurs on the back of solid athletic development, the biggest differentiator comes from those players who can propel their body with maximal intent, as opposed to those who both mentally and physically operate at a sub-maximal output.

- **Get fast:** Speed wins in sport. It is that simple. However, this supreme commodity has to be trained and managed. There is a genetic influence on a players' ability to be fast so we will always be constrained by this but speed must be used appropriately and protected from fatigue.
- **Maintain or peak:** Once we have looked to develop all the above we then cycle through working at all of them, at differing levels dependent on the season. We want players to peak for those all important match situations yet maintain sharpness through the lesser ones. The challenge for all strength and conditioning coaches is primarily the development of physical characteristics, secondly the maintenance and finally knowing when and how to take that player to the next level.

PRESCRIPTION OF SETS AND REPETITIONS

Exercise can be prescribed on a programme through both sets and reps, for example 'three sets of five repetitions' on a back squat (often written as back squat 3 × 5). Repetitions are individual lifts that, when performed one after another, form a set. So, doing five back squats in a row would form set one. The player then rests and performs set two and so on. There is generally an inverse relationship between sets and reps as there is volume and intensity. We would fatigue and break down if we carried out high volumes and high intensity. Conversely, we would struggle to elicit any adaptation with low volume and low intensity.

Fig. 5.9 shows some basic guidelines on loading for specific adaptations. There are many combinations of training and strategies for specific adaptations so the information is not exhaustive. The important thing for a coach is to find what works within your environment and constraints, and realistically what you have found to work anecdotally. Just as in other parts of life, individualization means some methods work better on some players than on others. While in the early stages there is a large amount of simplicity and generic programming, in the elite trained end of the spectrum you have the opportunity not only to work a little off-script but get a deep understanding of your players and how to get the most out of them. Just as the physiological systems adapt habitually and need progression, so too will your programming as you go on. The training journey should contain progressive content and look to challenge the players over time. In the early days, we will see general simple prescriptions of work that in time will no longer challenge. As a coach, you must decide when the player is ready to progress to more specific complex work. For the general population, the likelihood is they will never come near to a level of training years that requires anything earth-shattering.

LOADING OF EXERCISE

Assigning the correct load for players can be a challenging task as often a coach's ascertainment of a player's ability and his or her own can differ. In the early days, this process must be guided but over time players will become more involved in the training process and have a far greater involvement. It is also true to say setting loads for beginners is very difficult, simply by the fact players will make significant strength gains very quickly meaning any previous testing done to find maximum loads will soon become inaccurate. Untrained players will see significant early increases in strength as a result of increased neural drive (13) rather then any significant early structural changes. They are simply learning to hardwire efficient neural pathways and create a mind-muscle connection. Also, a lot of maximal testing is not necessarily appropriate for beginners from a safety perspective. We cannot use a mantra of 'technique before loading' as a coach and then try to expose a player with very little resistance training experience to maximal work. As

a result, I do not advocate assigning load in untrained individuals. The weight on the bar will naturally increase as the training process is bedded in. It is probably realistic to say players will be able to accumulate at least one or two years' training before you even need to assign the load they should lift. Simply, it is neither needed nor an efficient and worthwhile practice prior to this. Once players are trained, however, assigning the correct load is one of the key elements around player management and recovery and, as a result, their ability to peak.

As previously discussed, the continual monitoring of the training process revolves around testing, then subsequent phases of planning, doing and reviewing. By using 1RM testing with our trained athletes we can start to prescribe relative intensity based on percentages of players' maximal efforts. Fatigue accumulates through sets and it is important to assign the correct load to combat both the neural and structural effects of lifting to failure and the psychological toll it takes on players over time.

After appropriately carried out 1RM testing, we start to have a database of lifts and the maximums lifted by players. From that we must calculate loadings based on both the underpinning scientific recommendations (for example, three sets of five reps at 85 per cent of 1RM) and factoring in the inverse relationship between volume and intensity (Fig. 5.10).

For example, let us assume we have tested Player A and he has a squat 1RM of 100kg. That is to say, in his maximal testing 100kg was the maximum he was able to lift. Player A's programme states he will carry out four sets of five repetitions with an MH intensity (85–90 per cent relative intensity). Load would be assigned in the following manner:

100kg × 87.5% (RV for 5 repetitions) = 87.5kg
Medium heavy = 85–90% of Player A's repetition maximum
87.5kg × 85% = 74kg
87.5kg × 90% = 79kg

Volume (Reps)	% 1RM
1	100
2	95
3	92.5
4	90
5	87.5
6	85
7	82.5
8	80
9	77.5
10	75

Intensity	% 1RM
Very heavy (VH)	100
Heavy (H)	90–95
Medium heavy (MH)	85–90
Medium (M)	80–85
Medium light (ML)	75–80
Light (L)	70–75
Very light (VL)	65–70

Figure 5.10 Relative loading using volume and intensity.

Player A would therefore be looking to lift an MH range on five repetitions of back squat at 74–79kg.

One important note, specifically with a contact sport such as rugby, is that these guides are merely that. They do not take into account fatigue, soft tissue damage and the fact across a squad a game may have a more fatiguing effect on some players than others. Programming must always remain reactive to a degree, especially the more trained an individual becomes. It is not uncommon for a game played on soft ground with a high frequency of set piece instances to have a far greater fatiguing effect on forwards over backs, and thus a coach may need to take this into consideration. Likewise, different players fatigue at varying rates to their teammates. Some can tolerate higher volumes than others, or higher intensities. Programmes guide us, not constrain us. Use a common sense approach to understand when players need to grind through prescription for the greater good and when they need to take their foot off the gas a little. Over time as a coach, this will be a key skill in making sure players go into competition in top condition.

STRENGTH TRAINING EXERCISES

The strength programme you deliver should be progressive, appropriate to the individual and, above all else, balanced. If we are to train players with an 'athlete, sport, position' mindset then we have to prescribe programmes that create all-round gross athleticism. Sport is inherently unbalanced. We have hand dominance, foot dominance and in an open game situation such as rugby we have a multitude of scenarios that happen randomly. As a result, if we are to prevent injury and maintain a functional equality in structure we have to train both agonists and antagonists. Agonists are the prime movers, contributing the most to a specific action. Antagonists, on the other hand, act in opposition to the agonists. Rugby players have been known to have a tendency to overload one muscle group over another. Generally as a coach we have to combat players spending an inordinate amount of time training anterior dominant musculatures at the expense of the posterior chain. For example, players who favour a training regime built around anterior pressing exercises, such as the bench press on the assumption they are the muscles they see when they look in a mirror, over retraction and pull type exercises. These can have little correlation to athletic measures and can lead players to a higher likelihood of injury. The heavily developed anterior dominant player opens himself up to shoulder injury through tackle scenarios where the imbalance means he lacks range of motion when a player drives through a tackle and takes the arm and shoulder past the point where it can function safely. If the arm is taken to these further ranges there is often not the stabilization strength to maintain a stable shoulder joint, meaning players are more likely to suffer injury. Remember, as a coach your remit will always be to create balanced, multi-dimensional rugby players who have a wide range of force characteristics on which to call.

There are two main adaptations strength training should produce and this will vary at different times throughout the season and the training lifespan of a player.

- **Structural:** Structural benefits of strength training come from the hypertrophy of players' lean muscle mass. By increasing muscle size and, in turn, creating a larger cross sectional area, players will be able to produce more force. Although hypertrophy work is often seen as body-building type training, rugby needs an approach built around functional hypertrophy, where we increase size only to the musculature that contributes to rugby. A greater volume of muscle will aid protection for contact situations and form a foundation for prime mover muscles as we look to develop them as a precursor to other strength qualities. It is also worth noting that nutrition will play a key role in this process through protein re-synthesis.
- **Neural:** Neural adaptions occur as we get stronger and progressively overload training. Both inter- and intra-muscular coordination increases as a result, leading to an increase in the number of muscle fibres that can be recruited. The greater the number recruited, the more force we

can produce and therefore the stronger we become.

No matter what effect we are looking for from our programmes, technique will always drive their development. Loading a dysfunctional movement may appease the hearts and minds of players in the short term but will severely limit them in the long term. For that reason, as a coach you will need to have a wide menu of training options across any one squad for the simple fact there will be such a wide range of abilities within that group. Exercise prescription, while having one eventual destination in strength training, may have many different roads to get there. There is no hard and fast strategy to exercise regression and progression, although it is prudent to have one or two progressions and regressions for every main exercise group we have. Fig. 5.11 shows some example options, although as long as you are following the underpinning movement of each exercise, you can put your own exercise preferences in.

BODY WEIGHT TRAINING

The ability to control body weight is something that should be habitual to players, and all sportsmen and women for that matter. It is an area so often overlooked on the premise that lifting a load is more beneficial than no load. However, if we take strength training as a continuum that goes from general to specific, unloaded to loaded, it is a concern there is not more importance placed on it. While it should be a box that is ticked off early in the training journey, in most playing squads it still can form an integral part of warm-ups and ancillary work. All movements should be covered in programming (*see* Fig. 5.12) if the training is to be balanced.

A technical framework for all these exercises exists and should be hardwired into players through your coaching. Perhaps, of all the exercises, it is the body weight squat that will form the basis for most subsequent movements so it is an exercise that should

Main Exercise	Regression	Progression
Back squat	Body weight prisoner squat Counterbalance squat Squat to box	Increase load Alter 'time under tension' Isometric or paused reps Bands/chains
Romanian Deadlift	Hamstring curl Swiss ball hamstring curl Hip bridge SL cook hip lift	Increase load Single leg variations 'Good morning'
Single Leg Squat	Partial SL squat TRX assisted Step-up	Increase load Increase ROM Load through different planes
Bench Press	Press-up Wall press DB bench press	Increase load Alter 'time under tension' Isometric or paused reps Bands/chains
Pull-up	Lateral pull down Any horizontal pull Use bands to assist Eccentric lowers	Increase load Alter 'time under tension' Isometric or paused reps Bands/chains

Figure 5.11 How to progress and regress basic exercise.

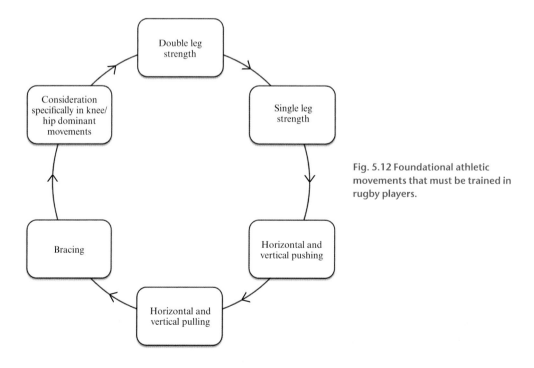

Fig. 5.12 Foundational athletic movements that must be trained in rugby players.

Fig. 5.13 Squat foot position.

Fig. 5.14 Knee alignment.

not only be ever present in programming but, moreover, the key technical points need to be both understood and executed by players. If any area of the movement breaks down it will have an impact further up the chain or lower down the body. If you were to ask your players to demonstrate five body weight squats it is likely you will see as many variations as you have players but this should not really be the case. Each key joint site should have a stand-ardized technical model and one, if you get right, that will transfer into all other lifts.

Foot position: Suggestions about the posi-tioning of feet seem to vary as to whether a player has been coached, left to their own devices or advised by sports medicine staff such as physios. First of all, what do we want to achieve? Eventually the squat will be loaded progressively with the overall goal of produc-ing high force lifting big loads. For that reason, we want a foot position that gives us the most solid base to do this. Too narrow and we will struggle to facilitate range of motion (ROM), too wide and we will be unstable and lose contribution from our prime movers. For this reason, positioning the feet so an imaginary line drops from the armpit to the inside of the ankle is favourable. The feet can be pointed outwards at an angle similar to a clock face

at five to one, or ten to two in taller or female athletes. The loading distribution of weight is also important. In the start position, the load is in the mid foot, moving to the rear of the foot in the descent and forward again in the ascent. At all times the whole sole of the foot remains flat in contact with the floor.

Knee alignment: The key with knee alignment is that the knees track straight, generally track-ing outwards slightly in line with the second to last toe on the foot. This outward position allows us to create a space so the hips can be dropped into vertically. At no point on the descent should we see a knee valgus, causing the knees to cave inwards. There are some cases, in very experienced lifters when the legs come inwards on the ascent to achieve a con-tribution from the adductor muscles, although, as a general rule, keep the knees straight and stable.

One of the greatest misconceptions is that the knee should not travel forward of the foot. It is impossible to do a squat without some forward movement of the knee and femur length, mobility and squatting style will also contribute to movement. If we look at the standard 'upright running' position (*see* Fig. 5.15), the knee moves over the toes as part of its natural movement.

Fig. 5.15 Standard upright position.

Fig. 5.16 Squatting.

The hamstring lengthens in the descent of a squat but if it is lacking in range it will pull the pelvis under in a posterior tilt. This could cause lumbar injury if the player loads weight through this incorrect position. Although the process of correction can be relatively straight-forward, it does not happen overnight and will involve a structured progressive programme of hip complex and lumbar spinal mobility and flexibility exercises.

The role the abdominal section plays in correct squatting technique is as a vital central support. In order to increase intra-abdominal pressure players need to brace the abdominal section. An effective tool for facilitating this is to have the player imagine they have in their abdomen a large coloured balloon. Prior to squatting, this balloon must be inflated by bracing. They must not only inflate it on an anterior/posterior axis but also on a lateral axis. By doing this, through abdominal bracing they are essentially creating stiff muscular buttresses in the intra-abdominal muscles allowing the spine to stay rigid. Through this one area we start to see why mid section control and strength are fundamental, not only to being strong and powerful, but to all athletic movement. If the chain has a weak link in the middle, the movement breaks down.

Hip complex/abdominal: The hip complex (in conjunction with the hamstrings) requires two main things. It needs stability to resist movement but also requires mobility to aid function and correct mechanics. In a squat, the hips and the knees 'break' or flex simultaneously so, when combined with a good wide foot position, it facilitates a space that the centre of mass can drop into vertically. Instability here can lead to the pelvis and hips tracking out of alignment, which could result in injury or compromise performance. A lack of mobility here commonly results in a posterior tilt.

Fig. 5.17 Hand positioning in body weight squat.

Thoracic and shoulder girdle: Correct postural alignment through the thoracic spine and shoulder girdle is important to allow the centre of mass to lower on a straight vertical line. The ability to maintain this posture comes first from a correct technical position, where the chest is held high and the shoulders are retracted. If there is an imbalance in programming, a player constrained by injury will struggle to retract the shoulders and under a loaded barbell will be pushed forwards, increasing pressure on the lower back and increasing the risk of injury.

Hand positioning: Finally, in the body weight squat, hand positioning can help assist the movement. Commonly, when you ask people to demonstrate what they believe is the correct technique they have their arms out in front. This is often as a result of the fact that, when we first teach the squat, we often use this method so the arms act as a counterbalance, assisting the movement. However, it can get people into bad habits as it forces the shoulders forwards and internally rotates both them and, as a result, the back. As shown above, we actually want the opposite of this to occur. The best solution is to interlink the fingers slightly and hold them behind the head. If the player then pulls the elbows back, retracting the shoulders and pulling the chest up, then he or she will maintain a better posture.

Posture: The squat, as with any other lift and technical position, is determined to a degree by the ability to maintain a good posture throughout the body. A good technical prompt in players is to get them to imagine they have a length of string from the centre of the sternum to the belly button. To maintain perfect posture, this imaginary string must be taut at all times. Whenever they perform a movement they must visualize the taut string. If at any time it loosens, they are curving the spine and the chest is dropping. In order to correct the posture and make the imaginary string tight again they simply lift the chest.

Breathing: This is an important consideration in lifting and overcoming resistance. It facilitates bracing, which will add structural stability to the lifts. Although there is a range of technical advice, with literature stating the breath is to be held and exhaled at key parts in the lift, a better course of action is to coach players to brace at the correct times as opposed to using breathing techniques. Intra-abdominal bracing will result in rigidity in the musculature, thus giving the spine the solidity it requires when moving load. The process of inhalation and exhalation will actually occur naturally as a result. We will breathe by the simple fact that, if we do not, we cannot function!

Body Weight Exercises

The body weight squat
Start position
– Position feet outside the shoulders, with a vertical line able to be dropped from the armpit to the inside of the ankle.
– Feet can be pointing outwards at an angle resembling '5 to 1' or '10 to 2' on a clock face.
– Abdominal muscles braced.
– Chest held high and shoulders retracted.
– Fingers interlocked behind the head with elbows drawn back by retracting the scapula.

Fig. 5.18 Body weight squat start position.

– Head in a neutral position, looking straight ahead.
– Weight should be on the mid foot.

Descent position

Fig. 5.19 Body weight squat descent position.

– Break at the hips and the knees simultaneously.
– As you descend, allow the knees to track outwards slightly following the line of the second smallest toe on each foot.
– Maintain a high chest, retracted scapula and lordotic curve in the back.
– Weight will move to the rear of the foot.

Bottom position

Fig. 5.20 Body weight squat bottom position.

– Descend so the point of the hip is lower than the point of the knee.
– Hold an upright torso maintaining the lordotic curve in the spine.
– In the lowest part of the descent, the weight will be firmly on the rear of the foot with the heel pushed into the floor.

Ascent position

Fig. 5.21 Body weight squat ascent position.

– Drive through the hips to allow the ankles, knees and hips to extend to a standing position.
– The weight will return to the mid foot.
– Remain braced throughout.

Single leg squat (from box)
There is a multitude of variation on single leg squats. The use of the arms as a counterbalance and a box to lower from help achieve a better position.

Start position
– Set a box/bench at a height appropriate to lower from. The heights can be graded as to the ability of the player, with lower heights being used in beginners and higher heights in the more experienced.
– Stand with one leg hanging to the side, ready to lower.

Fig. 5.22 Single leg squat start position.

- Put the arms out straight ahead.
- Chest should be held high, with scapula retracted.
- Abdominals braced.

Descent position
- The leg is held forward at an angle as the player descends.
- Maintain a flat back position as flexion at the hip and knee occur simultaneously.

Fig. 5.23 Single leg squat descent position.

- The arms remain outstretched as a counterbalance.
- The knee tracks in a straight line over the toes.
- Descend to a depth whereby the point of the hip is lower than the point of the knee.

NB: This is a challenging exercise and will prove difficult if there is not the required flexibility, stability and strength. More than likely, as a coach you are going to be required to apply regressive versions (namely in depth) as part of the coaching process.

Ascent position

Fig. 5.24 Single leg squat ascent position.

- The player extends through ankle, knee and hip to return to a fully upright, standing position.
- Abdominal muscles remain braced.

Cook hip lift
Start position
- Lie on the floor making sure the abdominals are 'drawn in' and the lumbar spine is flat.

Fig. 5.25 Cook hip lift start position.

- Bend in leg at the knee to 90 degrees and place the heel into the floor.
- Raise the other knee to 90 degrees and brace the abdominal muscles.
- Both feet should be pulled upwards in a dorsiflexion position.

Ascent position

Fig. 5.26 Cook hip lift ascent position.

- Driving the weight through the heel, extend the hips vertically.
- The body should be extended until it maintains a straight, rigid position.
- The non-supporting leg remains in place.

Press-up
The press-up is as much a test of stability, and the ability to brace the whole body, as it is a horizontal push exercise. As with most body weight exercises, it can be progressed and regressed by simply changing the angle, and thus increasing/reducing the load through the musculature. In the picture we have incline (easy), standard (medium) and decline (difficult) press-ups.

Start position

Fig. 5.27 Start positions for incline, standard and decline press-ups.

Fig. 5.27 (continued).   Fig. 5.28 (continued).

- Hands spaced shoulder width apart, fingers pointed forwards.
- Shoulders braced with elbows held in close to the body.
- Abdominals and glutes braced allowing for a straight body alignment.

Descent
- Remaining braced, lower downwards maintaining straight alignment.
- Shoulders remain stabilized and held close in to the body.

Ascent

Fig. 5.28 Descent positions for incline, standard and decline press-ups.

Fig. 5.29 Ascent positions for incline, standard and decline press-ups.

Fig. 5.29 (continued).

Start position

- Drive purposefully back to the start position, with the load concentrated down through the hands.
- Maintain braced alignment.

Row

As with the press-up, the row is a test of both stability and horizontal pulling. The exercise can be progressed and regressed using angles. There is also an opportunity to experiment with different grip positions and equipment, such as the use of ropes, suspension trainers and so on.

Fig. 5.30 Row start positions.

- Grip the bar a shoulder width apart with an overhand grip.
- Maintain a rigid, braced torso.
- Keep elbows in tight to the body.
- Squeeze the scapula downwards.

Ascent

Fig. 5.31 (continued).

- Lower the body back down to the start position in a controlled movement.

Airplane
Start position

Fig. 5.31 Row ascent positions.

Fig. 5.32 Start position for airplane.

- Retract the scapula.
- Row the body upwards maintaining alignment.
- At the top of the movement the bar should sit along the middle of the chest.

- Stand on one leg with the suspended leg a few centimetres off the floor.
- The support leg should have a 'soft knee' as opposed to the joint being locked.
- Hold the arms up, retracting the scapula and holding the chest high.

Descent

Fig. 5.33 Airplane descent position.

- The movement involves a hinging pattern at the hip joint.
- Keep the support leg stable and flex forwards, hinging at the hip.
- As you lower you must keep the chest high and shoulders retracted.

The non supporting leg is held rigid out behind the body with the player pushing through the heel.

Ascent

Fig. 5.34 Airplane ascent position.

- The player returns to the start position maintaining a rigid alignment, like a see-saw.

Loaded Lower Body Strength Exercises

The back squat

Fig. 5.35 Back squat rack position.

Rack position
- The barbell should be set at a height in the rack so a player can come under the bar, extend up a few centimetres and remove it. Bars that are set too low or too high increase the risk of injury.
- The player should grip the bar with an overhand closed grip, with the elbows at roughly 90 degrees. Note, larger players and those constrained by thoracic mobility issues may feel more comfortable with a slightly wider grip.
- The player extends upwards, removes the bar and takes one step backwards.

Start position
- The scapula should be retracted and pressed downwards.
- Position feet outside the shoulders, with a vertical line able to be dropped from the armpit to the inside of the ankle

Fig. 5.36 Back squat start position.

- Feet can be pointing outwards at an angle resembling '5 to 1' or '10 to 2'.
- Abdominal muscles braced.

Descent

Fig. 5.37 Back squat descent position.

- Break at the hips and the knees simultaneously
- As you descend, allow the knees to track outwards slightly following the line of the second smallest toe on each foot.
- Maintain a high chest, retracted scapula and lordotic curve in the back.
- Descend so the point of the hip is lower than the knee.
- In the lowest part of the descent, the weight will be firmly on the rear of the foot with the heel pushed into the floor.

Ascent position
- Drive through the hips to allow the ankles, knees and hips to extend to a standing position.
- The weight will return to the mid foot.
- Remain braced throughout.

Overhead squat

This is an excellent exercise that can help highlight to what degree a player can coordinate the upper and lower body. A challenge flexibility wise, it is an exceptional tool with which to instil greater movement literacy in your players. However, it does have its limitations in that there is a limit to the loading capability of the lift, and thus it tends to get used more as a warm-up exercise.

It is also a vital derivative lift of any snatch-based movements and, as such, should form part of a player's syllabus, especially if there is the intention to Olympic lift (snatch, clean and jerk) at a later date.

Start position

Descent

Fig. 5.38 Overhead squat start position.

Fig. 5.39 Overhead squat descent position.

– The bar should be held directly above the crown of the head with a wide grip.

Grip width will alter dependent on arm length but as a guide players should grip the bar with as wide a grip as possible.
– Arms should be locked straight, with players externally rotating the shoulders by trying to 'pull the bar apart'.
– The scapula should be retracted and pressed downwards.
– Position feet outside the shoulders, with a vertical line able to be dropped from the armpit to the inside of the ankle.
– Feet can be pointing outwards at an angle resembling '5 to 1' or '10 to 2'.
– Abdominal muscles braced.

– Break at the hips and the knees simultaneously.
– As you descend, allow the knees to track outwards slightly following the line of the second smallest toe on each foot.
– Maintain a high chest, retracted scapula and lordotic curve in the back.
– Descend so the point of the hip is lower than the point of the knee.
– In the lowest part of the descent, the weight will be firmly on the rear of the foot with the heel pushed into the floor.
– The bar must track downwards in a straight line so the load is held down centrally through hip, knee and ankle.

Ascent
– Drive through the hips to allow the ankles, knees and hips to extend to a standing position.
– The weight will return to the mid foot.
– Remain braced throughout.

Fig. 5.40 Overhead squat ascent position.

– The bar should be racked across the front of the shoulders with hands spaced in a 'clean grip'.
– With a loose grip, lift the elbows up to 90 degrees. In doing so the bar should sit comfortably on the ridge created on the clavicle.
– The scapula should be retracted and pressed downwards.
– Position feet outside the shoulders, with a vertical line able to be dropped from the armpit to the inside of the ankle.
– Feet can be pointing outwards at an angle resembling '5 to 1' or '10 to 2'.
– Abdominal muscles braced.

Descent

Fig. 5.42 Front squat descent position.

– Break at the hips and the knees simultaneously.
– As you descend, allow the knees to track outwards slightly following the line of the second smallest toe on each foot.
– Maintain a high chest, retracted scapula and lordotic curve in the back.
– Descend so the point of the hip is lower than the point of the knee.

Front squat
While an effective squat variation, the front squat is also a derivative of the power clean. It is the finish position, thus players need to learn the movement. It also has the benefits of requiring a more upright torso position and a greater contribution from the back extensor muscles.

Start position

Fig. 5.41 Front squat start position.

– In the lowest part of the descent, the weight will be firmly on the rear of the foot with the heel pushed into the floor.
– It is important the elbows remain high throughout the lift to avoid losing the bar forward.

Ascent

Start position

Fig. 5.43 Front squat ascent position.

– Drive through the hips to allow the ankles, knees and hips to extend to a standing position.
– The weight will return to the mid foot.
– Remain braced throughout.

Split squat
These present a great opportunity to load single leg strength positions. Often neglected, a rugby player will almost always be required not only to support on one leg (locomotion) but crucially reduce and produce force in contact positions. The lift can be varied by elevating the front support leg or the rear, giving players advanced challenges and potential for wider adaptations.

Fig. 5.44 Split squat start positions.

- The player should grip the bar with an overhand closed grip, with the elbows at roughly 90 degrees. Note, larger players and those constrained by thoracic mobility issues may feel more comfortable in a slightly wider grip.
- The legs should be split in a wide split stance.
- It is best to imagine the feet are on skis and they split following the same linear plane of motion.
- If required, the front or rear foot is elevated.
- Hips remain facing forwards with the abdominals braced.

Fig. 5.45 (continued).

Descent

- The player descends straight down, without shifting forward excessively.
- The torso must remain upright.
- The load on the support leg should load directly through the heel of the foot. Players should not allow the load to be directed forward into the knee.

Ascent
- Remaining braced and stable throughout, drive upwards, returning to the start position.

Fig. 5.45 Split squat descent positions.

Fig. 5.46 Split squat ascent positions.

Fig. 5.46 (continued).

Reverse lunge
Start position

Fig. 5.47 Reverse lunge start position.

– The player should grip the bar with an overhand closed grip, with the elbows at roughly 90 degrees. Note, larger players and those constrained by thoracic mobility issues may feel more comfortable in a slightly wider grip.

Descent

Fig. 5.48 Reverse lunge descent position.

– Remain braced in the abdominals.
– Take a large step backwards. The step should be large enough so in the lowest position the load is directly through the support foot.
– The upper body should remain upright and rigid.

Ascent

Fig. 5.49 Reverse lunge ascent position.

– Forcibly drive upwards to return to the start position.

Step-up

A box or bench can be used to offer different heights. The higher the box, the greater the challenge. It is likely to take players a while to build up to the top heights.

Start position

Fig. 5.50 Step-up start position.

Fig. 5.51 Step-up ascent positions.

– The bar should be held in a back squat position.
– The leg should be placed on a box so the point of the hip is lower than the point of the knee, replicating a deep squat angle.
– The foot should be flat with the weight distributed evenly.

Ascent
– Loading into the raised leg, drive upwards to the box.
– The movement should be controlled and not rely on too great a push-off from the rear leg.
– Remain braced with the hips and chest holding a neutral 'high' position.

– To add a greater stability/postural challenge, the knee can be driven up to 90 degrees, with the foot dorsiflexion.

Descent
– Lower back to the floor in a controlled manner.

– Repetitions may be done consecutively on one side or alternating between right leg and left leg.

Deadlift

While there are many variations of the deadlift, the example here shows a weightlifting deadlift. It replicates the lifting of the bar from the floor in a clean or snatch. By teaching this initial movement, we can both save time later and increase our ability to lift from the floor in the subsequent Olympic lifts.

If players are challenged mobility-wise or are especially tall then boxes can be used to set the bar at a slightly higher start position. Long term, though, the desire will be to get all players lifting from the floor effectively.

Start position

Fig. 5.52 Deadlift start position.

– The start position is vital as any technical deficiencies here will impact on the later stages of the lift.
– Grip should be just wider than the shoulders.
– Feet hip width apart.

– Grip wider than shoulder (thumb length).
– Shoulders over the bar.
– 'Chest up' and shoulders back. The back is squeezed to give a lordotic curve).
– Hips higher than knees.
– Bar should be over the top of the shoe laces or metatarsal-phalangeal joint (MPJ).

Ascent

Fig. 5.53 Deadlift ascent positions.

– Remove 'slack' from the bar.
– Extend knees and hips to lift the bar. Knees back.
– Angle of the back remains constant with the floor.

- Hips do not rise before shoulders.
- Bar remains as close to the body as possible.
- As the bar reaches past the knee, the hips extend forward towards bar.
- Body becomes more upright as hips extend through.
- Bar close to the body in contact with thighs.
- Arms remain locked straight, with the chest held high and the scapula retracted.

Descent

Fig. 5.55 Romanian deadlift start position.

Fig. 5.54 Deadlift descent position.

- The same process is followed to return the bar to the floor.
- It is important technique remains and the body stays braced to avoid poor positioning and injury.

Romanian deadlift
Start position
- Grip the bar in a 'clean' grip held at the waist.
- Feet shoulder width apart.
- The chest is held high with the scapula retracted.
- The knees are 'soft' and not locked.

Descent

Fig. 5.56 Romanian deadlift descent position.

- Hinging at the hip joint, bow forwards to a point where the spine is just above parallel with the floor. There is no need to go lower if the correct technique is being demonstrated. Some players will invariably feel this

93

a real challenge through a lack of hamstring flexibility. In time, this range of motion will increased if addressed appropriately.

− The hips should be pushed backwards so the load is in the heels.
− The player should feel tension in the glute complex and the hamstrings as opposed to the lower back.

Ascent

Fig. 5.57 Romanian deadlift ascent position.

− To return to the start position extend through the hips, remaining braced to a standing position.

Single leg Romanian deadlift
Start position
− Grip the bar in a 'clean' grip held at the waist.
− Stand on one leg with the suspended leg a few centimetres off the floor.
− The support leg should have a 'soft knee' as opposed to the joint being locked.
− Hold the arms up, retracting the scapula and holding the chest high.

Fig. 5.58 Single leg Romanian deadlift start position.

Descent

Fig. 5.59 Single leg Romanian deadlift descent position.

- The movement involves a hinging pattern at the hip joint.
- Hinging at the hip joint, bow forwards to a point where the spine is just above parallel with the floor.
- The hips should be pushed backwards so the load is in the heels.
- The player should feel tension in the glute complex and the hamstrings as opposed to the lower back.

Ascent

Fig. 5.60 Single leg Romanian deadlift ascent position.

- To return to the start position, extend through the hips, remaining braced to a standing position.

Loaded Upper Body Strength Exercises

The bench press
Ironic as it is, the most sought after rugby club record of the 'strongest bench presser' actually has little correlation with overall athletic ability. Biomechanically, it does not really reflect any rugby specific position other than getting up off the floor yet a disproportionate amount of time is spent training it. That being said, it is a straightforward upper body horizontal push exercise that has the ability to be manipulated throughout the force-velocity curve and thus has merit in some programming.

Start position

Fig. 5.61 Bench press start position.

- Lie on the bench making sure there are five points of contact with the body, head, shoulders, lower back, bottom and feet (on the floor).
- The bar should be gripped just slightly wider than shoulder width with a closed overhand grip.
- Brace the body, lift the bar from the rack and hold it vertically, with locked arms. The bar should line up with the mid chest.

Descent
- Lower the bar in a straight, controlled manner to the chest.
- Keep the elbows in close to the body and prevent them 'winging' outwards.
- Keep the abdominals braced.

Fig. 5.62 Bench press descent position.

Behind the neck press
Start position

Fig. 5.64 Behind the neck press start position.

Ascent

- Set up the bar as you would a back squat and remove from the rack.
- Knees should be soft, with the abdominals braced.

Ascent

Fig. 5.63 Bench press ascent position.

- Push the bar back up forcefully until the arms are vertical.
- Resist any movement in the bar, at all times keeping a straight plane of motion.

Fig. 5.65 Behind the neck press ascent position.

- Keeping the scapula retracted, squeeze the elbows in towards the back.
- Push the bar vertically until at a point where the arms should be extended fully.
- At the top of the movement the bar should be positioned above the crown of the head.
- The movement should be controlled, without assistance from a dip and drive from the lower body.

Descent
- The bar should be returned to the start position in a controlled manner, with care not to bang the bar off the top of the spine.

Single arm dumb-bell bench press
Dumb-bells are an effective alternative to barbells in push exercises. Requiring greater stabilization and intramuscular coordination, they offer greater injury prevention benefits.

Start position

Fig. 5.66 Single arm dumb-bell bench press start position.

- Lie on the bench making sure there are five points of contact with the body, head, shoulders, lower back, bottom and feet (on the floor).

- The dumb-bell should be gripped with a closed overhand grip and held with a fully extended arm.
- Brace the body and allow the arm not in use to rest on the leg.

Descent

Fig. 5.67 Single arm dumb-bell bench press descent position.

- Using a controlled action, lower the dumb-bell until it sits next to the chest but is not resting on it.
- Because of the unilateral demands of the lift, a large effort must be taken to stabilize the midsection and prevent excessive movement.

Ascent
- Remaining braced abdominally, push the dumb-bell back to the start position in a controlled, straight plane of motion.

Single arm push press
Start position
- Stand with feet shoulder width apart.
- Hold the dumb-bell with a neutral grip, taking care not to rest it on the shoulder.
- Keep the abdominals braced and maintain a straight vertical and horizontal alignment.

Fig. 5.68 Single arm push press start position.

Ascent

Fig. 5.69 Single arm push press ascent position.

- Maintaining the same alignment, dip the legs to a quarter squat position.
- Extend the hips purposefully, driving the dumb-bell vertically above the head.
- Stabilize the shoulder to prevent excessive movement of the dumb-bell.

Descent
- Using a controlled action, lower the dumb-bell until it sits next to the shoulder but is not resting on it.

Pull-up
The ability to pull body weight vertically should be a fundamental strength skill but it is an area that players often neglect. While certain positions such as front five players can struggle, nevertheless all players should be comfortable handling their own body weight. Players can experiment with different grips. Those who are yet not proficient can use elastic power bands as assistance, effectively reducing the load to be pulled.

Start position

Fig. 5.70 Pull-up start position.

- Grip the bar with an overhand closed grip, slightly wider than shoulder width apart.
- You should be in a 'dead hang' position with the arms extended fully.
- The body should be braced throughout.

Ascent

Fig. 5.71 Pull-up ascent positions.

– Pull the body upwards in a controlled motion.
– Pull to a point where the jawbone is above the bar.

Descent
– Lower the body in a controlled motion until the arms are extended fully.

Bent over row

Fig. 5.72 Bent over row start position.

Start position
– Start in the same position as the Romanian deadlift.
– Flex forwards at the hips so the body is parallel with the floor.
– Grip the bar with an overhand closed grip.
– The bar should be in line with the mid chest.

Ascent
– Retract the shoulders as the bar is drawn upwards.
– Pull until the bar meets the chest, maintaining the retraction in the scapula.

Fig. 5.73 Bent over row ascent position.

Fig. 5.74 Overhead med ball throw start position.

Descent
– Lower the bar in a controlled motion until the arms are fully extended.

Medicine ball exercises
Although medicine balls can be used in a variety of resistance exercise settings, it is as a precursor to Olympic lifts or as a stand alone explosive exercise variation where they deliver their most benefit. Both easy and safe to use, throwing in different planes of motion can help develop the powerful extension at the ankle, knee and hip, which is so fundamental to explosive movement.

Overhead medicine ball throw (from floor)
Start position
– The ball should be placed on the floor between the legs.
– Squat down and hold the ball with extended arms.
– The back should remain flat, the chest high and the scapula retracted.

Position 2

Fig. 5.75 Overhead med ball throw position 2.

– Drive upwards with maximal intent, extending at the hip.
– Maintain back alignment with the floor.
– Arms should remain extended fully as long as possible, ensuring a full extension of the hips.

Position 3

Fig. 5.77 Overhead med ball throw hang.

Fig. 5.76 Overhead med ball throw position 3.

– When the body is extended fully vertically at ankle, knee and hip, raise the arms above the head.
– Release the ball over the head.

Overhead medicine ball throw (hang)
– The technical points are the same as the throw from the floor, only the throw begins in a 'hang' position from the knee.

Kneeling medicine ball throw
Throwing from kneeling is another good variation. By taking out the contribution of the lower leg, there is greater explosive extension required from the hip complex to ensure full extension.

Explosive medicine ball push press
Start position
- Hold the medicine ball on the front of the body at the chest.
- The hands should be gripped firmly around the ball, in such a position that they are able to press the ball upwards.

Fig. 5.78 Explosive med ball push press.

- Keeping braced abdominally, dip the legs to a quarter squat depth while keeping the body upright.
- Drive explosively upwards and press the ball upwards in a straight line.
- As the ball moves upwards, the player should be extended fully.

Explosive Loaded Exercises
These include ballistic jumping type exercises, special strength training exercises, such as Olympic lift derivatives, and finally the Olympic lifts themselves.

Olympic lifts for players who possess the correct physiology, motor skill and training levels are a great tool for increasing force production and the rate of force production in players. They are challenging lifts that require significant technical and neural development but can produce excellent adaptations with regard to explosive ability. Their specificity lies in the biomechanical and neural correlation with sprint and jumping activities. The main benefit from the lift lies in the following adaptations:

- The lifts train athletes to explode using the maximum possible force in the shortest possible time.
- They produce a high rate of force development, a key point in sports training.
- Improved fast twitch muscle recruitment, primarily responsible for athletic ability.
- Hypertrophy of fast twitch muscle fibres.
- Development of efficient motor programmes.
- Improved capacity for explosive work.

With regard to training rugby players, it is important to assess the player in front of you and consider the benefit of the Olympic lifts. They take time to develop, which may not be a viable option with the time you have. Also, the lifts in their purest sense with a full squat catch at the floor are not essential unless time allows. For that reason, it serves well to coach the lifts into the 'power' position. While there is certainly a little less benefit than the full lift, it is a common sense and timely approach to maximize the effects.

As a caveat, however, the Olympic lifts are not essential should a coach wish to employ a different approach. They are essentially just jumping with a weight (so progressively overloading the unloaded jump pattern) and for that reason there are numerous alternative lifts you can use.

The jump squat
Start position

Fig. 5.80 Jump squat descent position.

Fig. 5.79 Jump squat start position.

- Unrack the bar and assume the same start position for a traditional back squat.
- Remember, this will be an explosive lift and the load on the bar should reflect this in your programming.

Descent
- Flex at the knees, dropping to a height you feel optimal for an explosive jump. This will be individual across players but it is unlikely they will drop below parallel.
- Remain braced with firm grip on the bar.

Ascent

Fig. 5.81 Jump squat ascent position.

- Extend explosively at ankle knee and hip and jump off the floor, keeping the legs straight. Players should be encouraged to 'push into the floor'.
- The landing will be determined by whether the lift is programmed as single lifts or continuous. Single lifts should land with a 'stick'

position, similar to the basic jump and land position seen in basic plyometric development. Multiple jumps will have a safe, stable position and will be programmed only when the player is at the required technical level.

Jump and shrug

This exercise is great for developing the powerful vertical extension in all the Olympic lifts, as well as being a good stand-alone exercise.

Start position

Fig. 5.82 Jump and shrug start position.

- Grip the bar in a clean manner.
- The grip should be a secure, overhand, closed grip.
- Feet pointed forward, no wider than hip width apart.
- Hold back posture by keeping shoulder blades back, chest up.

Position 2
- Slide bar a little way down the thigh while maintaining back posture and arms long.
- Bend comes from knees and hips with shoulders over the bar.

Fig. 5.83 Jump and shrug position 2.

Position 3

Fig. 5.84 Jump and shrug position 3.

- Extend forcefully through the hips, knees and ankles to straighten the legs and leave the floor.
- While in the air, shrug the shoulders by trying to touch the ears with the tops of the

shoulders. It is useful to use the coaching cue 'aggressive shrug' so there is maximal intent and, as a result, higher bar speed.
– Arms remain straight throughout movement with elbows turned out.
– Bar stays close to chest throughout movement.

Drop snatch

The drop snatch is great for developing the speed a player can get under the bar in a snatch-based exercise and his or her ability to land and stabilize. Remember, we need players who cannot only produce force but also reduce it.

Start position

Fig. 5.85 Drop snatch start position.

– Rack the bar on the shoulders as you would for a back squat.
– The hands must be placed wide, in a snatch grip.

Position 2
– Keeping a straight body alignment, extend up on to tiptoe.
– The player then drops down towards the floor, flexing at the ankle, knee and hip.

Fig. 5.86 Drop snatch position 2.

– As they drop, the bar should be driven up vertically and will finish above the crown of the head.
– The feet open out to a wider, stable position.
– At the bottom of the lift, the player will stabilize and stop. They will be holding the bar in what looks like the bottom portion of an overhead squat.
– The player then stands as they would in an overhead squat, returning to a standing position.

Drop clean

This follows a similar process but is built around getting players under the bar in a clean based lift.

Start position
– The bar is held in a power clean grip, the player stands upright with shoulders back. Feet pointed forward, no wider than shoulder width apart.
– The bar is lifted up to chest height keeping it close to the body.
– The player extends up on to tiptoe.
– Elbows remain high and stay above the bar.

Fig. 5.87 Drop clean start position.

Power shrug

Players can generally see good increases in the power shrug and in a relatively short time can start moving high loads with maximum intent. For that reason it is practical and easy to coach an exercise that forms part of any explosive lifting programme. The lift, as with many derivatives of the Olympic lifts, can be carried out with either a clean or snatch grip depending on what the coach decides most applicable.

Start position

Fig. 5.89 Power shrug start position.

Position 2
- Once the bar is at chest height, drop underneath it quickly 'snapping' the elbows under into a front squat position.
- The hips drop down and the feet 'scoot' out to a wider base, as would be adopted when performing a front squat.
- Stand back up with a controlled and balanced posture.

– Depending on the chosen grip, the bar will be held at mid thigh (the clean grip) or in the inguinal groove under the waistband (the snatch grip).
– The shoulders should be positioned slightly over the bar by bowing forward and flexing at the hip a little.
– Keep the head facing forwards in a neutral position and shoulders retracted.

Position 2
– Extend forcefully through the hips, knees and ankles to straighten the legs. Because of the increased load on the bar, the player will

Fig. 5.88 Drop clean position 2.

Fig. 5.90 Power shrug position 2.

Fig. 5.91 Hang clean start position.

not leave the floor but rather will be up fully extended on the balls of the feet.
– Shrug the shoulders aggressively.
– Arms remain straight throughout movement with elbows turned out.
– Bar stays close to the body throughout movement.

The hang clean

Lifts from the 'hang' position refer to a bar positioning above the knee, 'hanging' rather than starting from the floor. The hang clean can be simplified in coaching cues as simply a 'jump . . . shrug . . . and catch'.

Start position
– Keep bar close to thighs as body bows forward at the hips.
– Chest out, shoulder blades back.
– Lordotic curve in lower back.
– Postural muscles active.

Position 2
– This phase has the powerful triple extension and the jump phase.
– Hips, knees and ankles extend forcefully.
– Elbows rise up with the bar.

Fig. 5.92 Hang clean position 2.

– Shoulders are shrugged.
– Bar stays close to chest.

Position 3
– The lift finishes with the catch phase.
– Body drops under the bar.
– Elbows 'snap' under bar.
– Bar is 'racked' on top of shoulders.

Fig. 5.93 Hang clean position 3.

Fig. 5.94 Hang snatch start position.

- Hips are taken back and bar is caught in a front squat position.
- Feet land flat.
- Grip relaxed with bar on finger ends.

The hang snatch

Very similar in fundamental mechanics to the hang clean, the hang snatch can be cued as 'jump . . . shrug . . . throw'. A much faster lift, players often struggle to lift the same as clean variations.

Start position
- Keep bar close to thighs as body bows forward at the hips.
- Chest out, shoulder blades back.
- Lordotic curve in lower back.
- Postural muscles active.

Fig. 5.95 Hang snatch position 2.

Position 2
- Hips, knees and ankles extend forcefully.
- Elbows rise up with the bar.
- Shoulders are shrugged.
- Bar stays close to chest.

Position 3
- Body drops under the bar.
- Elbows 'snap' under bar to catch with arms fully extended.
- Hips are taken back out and bar is caught in an overhead squat position.
- Feet land flat.

Fig. 5.96 Hang snatch position 3.

Clean/snatch pull
Start position

Fig. 5.97 Clean/snatch pull start position.7

- Feet hip width apart.
- Grip overhand wider than shoulder (thumb length).

- Chest up and shoulders retracted. Shoulders and back are braced to give a lordotic curve.
- Hips higher than knees.
- Elbows rotated outwards.
- Bar positioned close to the body and over the MPJ (metatarsal-phalangeal joint).

The first pull

Fig. 5.98 Clean/snatch first pull position.

- Remove 'slack' from the bar.
- Extend hips and knees to raise the bar, knees back.
- Angle of the back remains constant with the floor.
- Chest remains high.
- Hips do not rise before the shoulders.
- Bar remains as close to the body as possible.
- 'Push the platform away'.

Transition phase (or scoop)
- Key phase as the re-bending of the knees (double knee bend) gives us the eccentric phase before the concentric, thus assisting in the plyometric nature of the lift. It is here the stretch shortening cycle (SSC) occurs.
- As the bar passes the knee, the hips extend/ drive forward towards it. This part of the lift can also often be called the scoop.

Ready to jump position

Fig. 5.100 Power clean start position.

Fig. 5.99 Clean/snatch pull ready to jump position.

- Body becomes more upright.
- Bar in contact with mid thighs (or inguinal groove).
- Arms are still straight.
- Aggressive triple extension of ankle, knee and hip.
- Shoulders to ears.

Power clean

Start position
- Feet hip width apart.
- Grip overhand wider than shoulder (thumb length).
- Chest up and shoulders retracted. Shoulders and back are braced to give a lordotic curve.
- Hips higher than knees.
- Elbows rotated outwards.
- Bar positioned close to the body and over the MPJ (metatarsal-phalangeal joint).

First pull position
- Remove 'slack' from the bar.
- Extend hips and knees to raise the bar, knees back.

Fig. 5.101 Power clean first pull position.

- Angle of the back remains constant with the floor.
- Chest remains high.
- Hips do not rise before the shoulders.
- Bar remains as close to the body as possible.
- 'Push the platform away'.

Transition

Fig. 5.102 Power clean transition position.

- Key phase as the re-bending of the knees (double knee bend) gives us the eccentric phase before the concentric, thus assisting in the plyometric nature of the lift. It is here the SSC occurs.
- As the bar passes the knee, the hips extend/ drive forward towards it. This part of the lift can also often be called the scoop.

Second pull

Fig. 5.103 Power clean second pull position.

- Body becomes more upright.
- Bar in contact with mid thighs.
- Arms are still straight.
- This is the power position and is basically a jump and shrug.
- Aggressive triple extension of ankle, knee and hip.
- Shoulders to ears.
- Elbows will raise up with the bar extending out along it.
- Bar remains in contact with body.

Catch

Fig. 5.104 Power clean catch position.

- Body drops fast under the bar.
- Elbows snap under.
- The bar is racked across the front of the shoulders.
- Hips are flexed back out and the bar is caught in a quarter front squat position.
- Elbows remain high with a relaxed grip.
- Feet land heavy and flat.

Power snatch

Fig. 5.105 Power snatch start position.

Fig. 5.106 Power snatch first pull position.

Start position
- Feet hip width apart
- Grip the bar in a wide snatch style.
- Chest up and shoulders retracted. Shoulders and back are braced to give a lordotic curve.
- Hips higher than knees.
- Elbows rotated outwards.
- Bar positioned close to the body and over the MPJ (metatarsal-phalangeal joint).

First pull position
- Remove 'slack' from the bar.
- Extend hips and knees to raise the bar, knees back.
- Angle of the back remains constant with the floor.
- Chest remains high.
- Hips do not rise before the shoulders.
- Bar remains as close to the body as possible.
- 'Push the platform away'.

Transition
- Key phase as the re-bending of the knees (double knee bend) gives us the eccentric phase before the concentric, thus assisting in the plyometric nature of the lift. It is here the SSC, or stretch shortening cycle, occurs.
- As the bar passes the knee, the hips extend/drive forward towards it. This part of the lift can also often be called the scoop.

Second pull

Fig. 5.107 Power snatch second pull position.

- Body becomes more upright.
- Bar in contact with the waistband (inguinal groove).
- Arms are still straight.
- This is the power position and is basically a jump and shrug.
- Aggressive triple extension of ankle, knee and hip.
- Shoulders to ears.
- Elbows will rise up with the bar extending out along it.
- Bar remains in contact with body.

Catch

Fig. 5.108 Power snatch catch position.

- Body drops fast under the bar.
- Elbows 'snap' under.
- The bar is racked across the front of the shoulders.
- Hips are flexed back out and the bar is caught in a quarter front squat position.
- Elbows remain high with a relaxed grip.
- Feet land heavy and flat.

Split jerk

Start position

- The bar is unracked from the stands/rack as you would for a front squat.
- The abdominals are braced keeping the body rigid and straight.

Position 2

Fig. 5.109 Split jerk position 2.

- The lift is initiated with a dip.
- Flex the knees to drop approximately 15cm.
- The angle of the upper body should remain upright.
- The elbows will drop slightly from 90 degrees to 45 degrees.

Position 3

- Extend the hips powerfully.
- Following the powerful extension, the legs are split forwards and backwards, looking like a split squat position.
- At the same time, the arms are driven up to full lockout and the body drops into the split pattern.

Fig. 5.110 Split jerk position 3.

Position 1

Fig. 5.111 Single arm dumb-bell snatch position 1.

– The bar should be directly above the crown of the head with the bar loading straight down through the centre of mass.

– Bow forward at the hips as you would in a Romanian deadlift.

It is important to note this explosive exercise is more about the speed of the movement to drop under the bar, rather than being about a big press of the shoulders.

Position 2

Single arm dumb-bell snatch

This is a good exercise to encourage an explosive full extension, yet is relatively easy to coach and requires less technical input. And, while it is harder to programme in higher loads, it can be useful in increasing the velocity end of the strength curve.

Start position
– Flexing at the hips and knees, hold the dumb-bell extended down between the legs.
– Keep the chest up and scapula retracted.

Fig. 5.112 Single arm dumb-bell snatch position 2.

– Extend powerfully at ankle knee and hip, sending the body upwards.

Position 3

Fig. 5.113 Single arm dumb-bell snatch position 3.

- Keeping the dumb-bell close to the body, allow the elbow to raise and move outwards along the line of the dumb-bell.
- Snap under so the dumb-bell is held above the head.

Mid Section and Trunk Stabilization Training

Stability in the mid section of the body, or trunk, plays a vital role in a player's ability to transmit force into the upper or lower body. Without this central core musculature transmitting forces effectively down into the ground, athletic ability will always be compromised. The player can be as strong in the extremities of the body as they like but they require a mid section that can direct forces produced and the amplitude at which they occur. Think of any positional skill in rugby and a weak mid section will have a negative effect. It may be a player crumpling in the middle on contact, or even a player's ability to slow down and change direction without the mid section bracing against breaking forces; core strength and stability is required. In short, a strong core allows force to be transferred through the legs to the arms smoothly and efficiently (14).

But what are we looking to really train? 'Core stability' training has seen numerous incarnations over the years and has often been subject to gimmicks and every piece of weird and wonderful equipment known to man. But rarely does it train the areas we require.

Essentially, players need to be able to mobilize the mid section, allowing rapid explosive movements that produce high force or power. Conversely though, holding posture, resisting gravity and stabilizing require strong stabilizing characteristics. As has become evident across all athletic movement, range of motion and mobility/movement are core skills that should be attained before overloading. If players cannot move freely through all movement planes, they will potentially be limited in their skill capacity but, even more so, imbalanced and an injury waiting to happen. Once movement is adequate though, the important concept a strength and conditioning coach must consider is resistance of movement through the mid section as opposed to producing movement. The ability to brace and resist movement abdominally is what allows force to be transmitted effectively into the ground or throwing activities.

The core should be considered as one interlocking global musculature that extends from the shoulders down to the knees. As a result, we should train it as such. We are looking to build strong buttresses, not only extending down the anterior, and posterior of the mid section, but also laterally. It is an area that is often neglected, with players favouring anterior flexion type exercises such as the abdominal crunch or back extensions exercises yet the muscle action is not consistent with the needs of the sport. If we look to track and field, where we have powerful fast athletes, we find in almost all of them the mid section has both breadth and depth in the musculature. It has to withstand reducing the forces of movement and in turn producing high forces in highly explosive athletic events.

As long as this concept of resisting movement is applied, the exercise choice is secondary and ultimately at the discretion of the coach. It is beneficial, however, to analyze some key rugby positions where trunk stability is essential and replicate the movements in a resistive stance. Likewise, key athletic and biomechanical positions can also be used in this way.

The positions below are an idea of how to challenge trunk stability. They can be added to warm-ups and work well as partner-assisted drills. In terms of prescription, time will be used over sets and reps. For example, 4 x 30 seconds.

Players should hold the positions and resist against partners trying to push and move them from different positions. This random approach builds great intra muscular coordination and stability and, as players become more proficient, they can look to be challenged with different stimuli such as unstable surfaces. The figures below show some basic positions that can be used.

Fig. 5.114 Four-point stance.

Fig. 5.115 Lateral star.

Fig. 5.116 Side plank.

Fig. 5.117 Scrum hold.

6

SPEED, AGILITY AND PLYOMETRIC TRAINING FOR RUGBY

Alongside both a comprehensive resistance programme and an appropriate metabolic conditioning programme, it is also the role of any good strength and conditioning coach to teach players to develop speed. As with the programming of resistance training, these much sought-after athletic qualities in players must follow a technical framework and be supported by a scientific rationale.

As with all sports, speed is not only a key determinant of success but also a unique quality that, when used effectively by players, can separate the winners from the losers. However, as with most athletic qualities, there is a degree of genetic influence on a player's capability to be fast and explosive. As coaches, we cannot simply make any player 'fast and explosive'. Sadly, for any player to be fast there has to be an underlying muscle physiology for us to even to see an application of speed. Players who possess both a high amount of fast twitch fibre and, crucially, the neural skill set to activate these fibres will have a predisposition to be fast, reactive and explosive. On the other hand, players who are predominantly slow twitch, or who cannot activate and coordinate the neuromuscular system in the correct manner, will find it impossible to ever become 'fast'. However, through an appropri-

ate training framework and an all-encompassing strength and conditioning programme, they can become 'faster' than they were. With that in mind, as coaches we need to develop the right physical and neural qualities in all our players to progress them within their capabilities.

Within rugby, and any multi-directional, ground-based sport, there are three key areas to develop:

- Plyometric ability – Simply the ability of players to move reactively using the mechanical and neuro-physical properties of muscle
- Linear speed – The ability of players to accelerate, reach and maintain top speed
- Agility – The ability of players to both reduce speed and produce it in game scenarios.

PLYOMETRICS

Plyometric training should form a portion of players' work once there has been a suitable volume of training experience. Such exercises are not suitable for untrained players and doing them incorrectly could be dangerous and also lead to poor technique, negating

117

Fig. 6.1 The three phases of plyometric activity.

any of the positive adaptations. Assuming the players are at an appropriate level, introducing plyometric training enables us to train the bottom of the force-velocity curve.

Plyometrics are a 'shock' method of training that enable muscles to reach maximum strength in a short as time as possible (1). These dynamic, explosive activities have three distinct phases that must be present for a plyometric response to occur and use the stretch shortening cycle (SSC). The SSC uses a combination of stored elastic energy created within the muscles and tendons (mechanical model) and the physiological stretch reflex of the muscle (neuro-physical model) to create a powerful concentric action. The SSC is time dependent and must occur in under 250m/s, and thus plyometric training will always also be time dependent.

Eccentric Phase: Fig. 6.1 illustrates the eccentric phase as the player lands. There is an eccentric muscle action whereby the muscle lengthens as there is flexion at the hip and knee joints.

Amortization phase: The most crucial element occurs on landing. The reactive ability of the player here dictates whether or not he or she can attenuate the force of the opposing ground here. The less time spent on the ground, the more reactive, and thus plyometric, the action will be.

Concentric phase: As a result of the opposing action of the floor and the stored elastic energy in the muscle, the player is propelled upwards explosively with an extension of the ankle, knee and hip.

The mechanical model: Elastic energy is stored up in the musculo-tendinous unit (MTU) in eccentric muscle actions. This arrangement of connective tissues, tendons and ligaments is vital in the release of stored elastic energy. This creates tension in the muscle and tendons, like when a piece of elastic is stretched. The most tension will occur when the MTU is rapidly stretched and it is the energy stored in this tension that allows the tendons to transmit force and facilitate explosive reactive movement. However, the faster this release occurs, the higher the rate of force that will be available. Imagine two identical players side by side looking to complete a vertical jump test. Assume the players are identical on a physical level (it is a hypothetical scenario!). Player A is going to complete the test jumping naturally and limiting the time spent in the bottom of his flexed position. He must flex to a self-selected depth that he feels instinctively will send him upwards as far as possible. Player B, on the other hand, is going to use a different strategy. He is going to flex (squat) as low as possible and hold the position for 10 seconds. Who will jump higher, Player A or Player B? Because it is

the rate of the stretch that occurs rather than the magnitude, Player A will jump higher. The longer Player B holds in the low positions, the more stored energy dissipates away. Plyometric actions are reactive and work only if the stored elastic energy is released immediately. They are driven by the motor skills of a player. Players therefore must be trained to use this energy efficiently and optimally. Train them slowly and these skills will not develop. Train too much at the force end of the strength curve and, again, the same will occur.

The Neuro-Physical Model

The stretch reflex that occurs, facilitating the stretch shortening cycle, is an involuntary response triggered from the muscle spindle held intra-muscularly. This muscle spindle is able to detect rapid stretches in the muscle, such as those when landing or changing direction. The involuntary response is a safety mechanism that is built into us to prevent a muscle over-stretching and, potentially causing injury. As a result of this, we have increased muscle action, meaning there is a greater ability for a more forceful concentric action. This works alongside the golgi tendon organ (GTO) situated in the musculo-tendinous junction. The GTO works on a sensory level detecting muscle change and tension and will also protect against muscle tension injuries. Therefore, increasing a player's plyometric ability will be important when it comes to maximizing the myotatic response of the muscle spindle, while inhibiting the GTO. In short, we have to overcome the natural safety mechanism of the human body otherwise plyometric movement will be impossible.

If this occurs we are likely to see:

- Increased activation in the fast twitch, high threshold motor units. It is these motor units that deliver the reactive explosive element and they need to be targeted and trained. Understanding the fundamental premise of plyometric activities and the timescale in which they should happen will guide exercise selection as a result. Be very careful in programming the correct exercise for the desired outcome. Like resistance training, just because something may look fast and specific, does not always mean that is what is happening. Box jumps, for example, look explosive and are often wrongly programmed as plyometric exercise. While a part of ballistic training, and a precursor to many true plyometric movements, they are not using the SSC in the correct timeframe and thus are not truly plyometric in their action

- Increased synchronization occurs as a player gains a greater aptitude for reactive plyometric jump work. It is a complex motor skill and must be given the time it requires. We can use a light bulb analogy and imagine the strength and power work our players are doing as being directly related to how bright bulbs glow when switched on. The stronger and more powerful a player, the higher the dimmer switch can be turned. The weaker a player, the lower the amount of available brightness available. Plyometric training, when done correctly, will allow greater synchronization. So the player can illuminate more bulbs, brighter, at a quicker rate

- Increased discharge rates for power exercises will be easier for the athlete to complete. It will give them a more balanced strength/speed/power profile and greater options on an athletic level.

Finally, training with plyometric exercise will lead to the disinhibition of the GTO, facilitating plyometric movement. This increases a player's ability to manipulate the physiological systems of the body.

Once the basic premise is understood, we must then look at how best to programme plyometric exercise into our training cycle. It is important to understand though that the complex nature of plyometrics, and the need to train in such a way as to optimize the neuro muscular system, means we should follow a framework. As with any skill, proficiency in the whole movement or skill needs to be trained and taught through mastering the individual components first.

We have already discussed the three stages of eccentric, concentric and amortization. But how can we simplify these to best develop the plyometric skills? As a framework (see Fig. 6.2), we want to develop the ability of players to land (eccentric action), take off (concentric action) and, crucially, to couple the two movements to rebound (reactive ability).

Exercise prescription should be considered as part of a long-term approach to developing the basic skills required and intensity and complexity of movement will come only on the back of this foundation. It can often be difficult for players to understand how some of the skills, such as landing, appear in their programme if they do not understand the skill. As a coach, this area must be educated if you wish players to learn what will be a complex skill for many. Too often, players and coaches see the drills as opposed to the movement. A basic plyometric progressive drill will deliver far more adaptations than the complex drill you see on the internet but you have to be prepared to educate the players as to why it will work. They will generally always be sidetracked by the false notion that:

- The most complicated drill delivers the best return
- They are in the physical condition to replicate it. The reality is most players possess neither the physical strength nor the neural skill to be effective at plyometric training until they are some way into their long-term training journey.

As stated, landing will always be the first thing to teach. Eccentric in its nature, it

Fig. 6.2 The technical framework for teaching plyometrics.

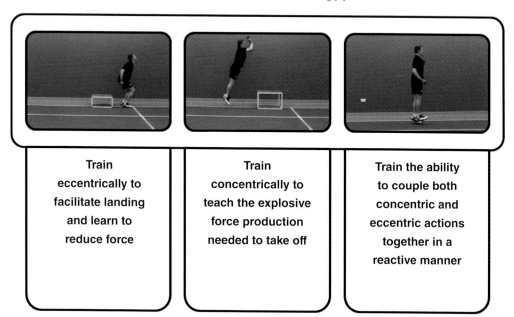

Train eccentrically to facilitate landing and learn to reduce force	Train concentrically to teach the explosive force production needed to take off	Train the ability to couple both concentric and eccentric actions together in a reactive manner

requires a player to tolerate the stretch load on landing, which in itself is a significant test of eccentric strength. Not only are we looking for players to be able to tolerate these loads, over time we want them to increase the loads. The less able they are to reduce force eccentrically, the less efficient they will be at landing and, as a result, the amortization timescale will increase. The longer this is, the slower the jump will be and the less likely it will initiate a fast stretch shortening velocity. Always remember, plyometric activity is time dependent. We are trying to combine both a physical and technical framework in our sessions that leaves our players with 'super stiffness'. It is this quality that will facilitate quicker, more explosive reaction. The player who reacts and moves quicker will always have the upper hand in sport.

We have stressed the importance of core control and strength in plyometric activity but there are also other skills your players will require. The key ones that will contribute to developing explosive, reactive players are:

- **Proprioception**: This refers to the body's ability to adapt and find equilibrium against changes in movement in the immediate environment. The better a player's ability, the greater the chance to beat the opposition through movement. This is even down to how the body adapts and deals with, for example, differing surfaces.
- **Coordinative skill**: Players need to coordinate a great deal both physically and on a skill level. While on a physical level we are looking for players coordinating their bodies and the neural system, it is the game scenario that then presents even more challenges. Players in games not only have to carry out a physical skill, such as changing direction, but have to do so adding the skill/tactical element of rugby and coordinate this around opposition activity.
- **Motor control**: The neural system must drive the physical system effectively to facilitate efficient movement.

- **Intent:** Plyometric movement will simply not be initiated without that maximal intent. If players need to be explosive, they must train explosive.
- **Spatial awareness:** In a game scenario, it is clear that players need to be spatially aware around their team, the opposition and the general environment.

Safety

It is important that before we actually programme specific exercises and drill we consider some basic safety areas that dictate whether or not plyometrics will be appropriate.

As with most training interventions, both biological age and training age are key. It is not uncommon to hear people discount the use of plyometric training with youngsters as dangerous and something to avoid. There are no issues with young players of any age partaking in jumping activity so long as they have a comprehensive training history. If they are strong enough, skilled enough and, crucially, stable enough they are fine to progress. The problem often arises, though, when players do not possess this foundational strength and they plough on regardless. Before very long they will be at an increased chance of injury, the last thing any coach wants. It is not uncommon for literature to state an individual should not carry out plyometric exercise until they can do a body weight squat with twice body weight. This is an outdated concept and, if it were the case, many players and athletes would be deemed too weak. Essentially, what we want are players who are strong enough relative to their body weight. We often see instances like this where players are deemed unsuitable for certain exercise choices. It is important to remember they will still be classed as safe to carry out the same movement in their sport, so why then can they not train in an applicable manner?

Body mass will also be a factor to consider. Rugby tends to have heavier individuals due to

positional requirements and the risks increase in these players.

Gender should be considered. Females can be at greater risk of injury at the knee as a result of their structural design. Wider hips increase what is called the Q angle, i.e. the angle of the hip to the knee. The greater the angle, the greater the instability when landing. Consequently this, aligned with females generally being weaker, means it may take some time before plyometric exercises are appropriate for the general female population.

Externally, the equipment and location need to be safe. Footwear should consist of a stable and secure training shoe. The surface should be firm and reactive, such as a track. Working in boots on a muddy pitch will not only increase injury but the external equipment will negate the effects of plyometric training.

Finally, the two most important considerations are warm-up and your ability as a coach. Plyometric training, and speed training in general, requires players to operate maximally at the higher ends of their ability. A thorough warm-up that prepares for the session is required. A few laps around a pitch and a few stretches are not going to prepare someone to land and jump explosively. The warm-up should be appropriate to the content of the session. As a part of this, you as a coach need to implement an environment and programme that allows for this. Plyometrics needs a large amount of coaching due to its technical nature.

Landing Exercises

When coaching landing mechanics we first want to ensure the foot strike is correct. As with all lifts and sprint activity where the body weight sits through, the foot can be the difference between an effective efficient movement and a slow, sub-standard action. Although slowed down it appears the optimal landing is with a flat foot, it is actually the mid foot that should be in contact in the landing. Loading

	Stationary Drills	Landing Horizontally	Landing Vertically	Landing Multi Directionally
Double Leg Landings	Tall soldiers jump + stick Drop stick	Broad jump + stick Hurdle + stick	Single jump + stick Multiple jump + stick Drop + stick drills	Same landings but done in a multi-directional pattern
Single Leg Landings	Hop + hold Walk + stop	SL hop + hold for distance SL hurdle Hop + hold	SL drop and stick	Same landings but done in a multi-directional pattern

Figure 6.3 A teaching progression for landing.

too much to the heel or the forefoot will compromise the effectiveness of the landing and see little contribution from the required musculature. It is important there is alignment down through the centre of mass, just like in a squat. After all, a squat is simply a slowed down regression of a jump. It uses the same mechanics and joint sites.

Landing effectively and the ability to do it in all directions regardless of level will be a mainstay of programmes. Not only will it allow players to better attenuate ground forces, it can also be used as an injury prevention tool. Think about where many injuries occur, it is in slowing down or changing direction. If we cannot reduce force, the ability to load eccentrically and reduce the speed at which the body is moving, we risk joint site injury specifically at ankle, knee and hip. To create an all-round rugby athlete we must implement this concept.

Landing drills can appear simple but coaches and players neglect them at their peril. As with any of the plyometric positions, Fig. 6.3 shows the simple parameters by which we should guide landing exercise selection. I think it is important to understand the exercise is secondary to the training concept. Anyone can devise exercises. Some will be appropriate if they follow the key principles, some will be time wasted if they do not. As a coach, always ask the question: what am I trying to achieve with this drill?

We are always going to teach relatively static landing drills first. Once mastered, we can increase both the complexity and the magnitude of the landings but always keep the drill simple and coach the movement. We are not trying to confuse players. We want to develop a skill that will translate to movement on the pitch.

NB: Players must be warmed up fully and possess appropriate strength levels before developing plyometrics.

Tall soldier
Start position
− Stand in a tall, rigid position like a soldier at attention.
− In your own time, drop fast into a quarter squat position.
− The feet can shoot out slightly and the landing should be braced with no subsequent bend at the knee.
− A beneficial coaching cue is to have players imagine they are dropping into glue; the position should be held as a 'stick' rather than a cushioning movement.

Fig. 6.4 Tall soldier.

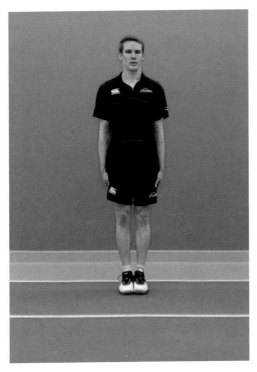

Drop and stick

Dropping from a height increases the magnitude of the stretch load eccentrically and the height of the box should only be increased in line with technical ability. The height of the box that a player drops from should be progressed from 'mid shin' to 'knee height' and then to 'mid thigh'.

The exercise can also be undertaken as a single leg (SL) variant, principally as in game scenarios most opportunities for a player to reduce force and movement of their body occur on one leg.

– Stand at the edge of the box.
– The foot is pre-activated in a dorsiflexed position.
– Step off the box and land in a flexed position, 'sticking' the landing. There should be no movement from the flexed knee position.

– The ankle, knee and hip should be aligned to replicate good squatting mechanics and there should be no movement of the knee joint inwards.
– The chest and shoulders should remain upright with a braced mid section.

Hop and hold

– Jump forward from a standing position.
– Land on one leg in a flexed position, 'sticking' the landing. There should be no movement from the flexed knee position.
– The knee must remain aligned with no movement.

The player should start these exercises with little distance covered, increasing horizontal distance or vertical distance over time.

Fig. 6.5 Drop and stick.

Progressions and Regressions of Landing

All the exercises follow basic technical points of landing mentioned above. To progress, we simply change the difficulty of the exercises by using increased distance. It is not appropriate in all bar the most gifted of athletes to add load, such as weighted vests. Conversely, if the exercises need regressing, the first area to address will always be basic strength work in the gym. If a player cannot perform the basic movements in static, gym-based exercises, they certainly would be able to show proficiency in a dynamic scenario. Shown below is a teaching progression that any player could travel through in their training programmes:

- Good all-round general conditioning, specifically with regard to optimal body composition.

- Proficiency in both double leg and single leg body weight strength exercises and the ability to repeat them (muscular endurance).
- Sufficient training history in loaded double leg and single leg strength exercises with attention given to challenging players eccentrically, concentrically and isometrically in exercise selection.
- In place landing.
- Low horizontal and low vertical landing.
- Low multi-directional horizontal and vertical landing for repeated jumps.
- Increased vertical, horizontal and lateral magnitude for repeated jumps.

Taking Off

Once we are happy players can reduce force effectively on landing, we can look to teach them how to jump up. Remember, just as with the Olympic weightlifting movements where we are asking players to jump with maximal intent, the same is true with jumping.

Without this intent and the assisted propulsion from the arms we are not going to see vertical movement. Obviously, levels of strength and power dictate this to a degree but so too does technique. Poor jumping technique is common, even with athletes from jump-based sports. It tends always to be a result of not using the arms to help propel the body upwards.

Again, we require this propulsion off both two legs and one leg so drills can be adapted to suit. Likewise, we can use an array of equipment to assist or challenge players; specifically boxes, mini hurdles, steps and so on.

Counter movement jump

The counter movement jump is a 'go to' exercise in the teaching progression for jumping up. The arms are fixed at the hips, so it helps develop that initial intent and maximal effort needed for an explosive jump. What depth players should descend to can be a frequent question. It is best to instruct players to descend to the depth that they instinctively feel is optimal to jump their highest. Too high and they will not use the stretch response or the lower body musculature. However, too low and the time is increased resulting in a potential loss of stored energy, which will subsequently affect the jump.

Players will tend to fall in the category of either 'hip jumper' or 'knee jumper'. Hip jumpers seem to need little depth, relying more on hip extension to send them upwards. Knee jumpers, on the other hand, need to use the greater depth to jump high.

Start position
- Stand with feet shoulder width apart. The hands are placed on the hips.
- Descend to your individual depth then extend explosively from ankle, knee and hip.

- The player remains straight and tall in the air, keeping the legs straight.
- The toes come up to their neutral anatomical position.
- On landing, 'stick' the movement as with the landing drills.

Vertical jump
- Stand with feet shoulder width apart. The hands are placed by the side.
- Descend to your individual depth with the arms swinging behind the body. Extend explosively from ankle, knee and hip.
- The arms swing forwards and propel the body upwards. At the fully extended point, the arms should be pointing straight up.
- The player remains straight and tall in the air, keeping the legs straight.
- The toes come up to their neutral anatomical position.
- On landing, 'stick' the movement as with the landing drills.

Jumping up to box
The heights of the box that a player drops from should be progressed from mid shin to knee height to mid thigh to waist and so on. The box or platform that a player is landing on must be stable and appropriate for his or her body weight.

It is also worthwhile when players are jumping on to a box with a height above the knee that a box half its height is placed next to it. Injury can occur from repetitive jumping or stepping down from high heights and the smaller box allows for a safer, more manageable, return to the floor:
- Start from an appropriate distance away from the box, allowing for the feet to be able to clear the edge.
- Descend and then extend fully as you would on a vertical jump, driving explosively with the arms.
- Jump up and land on the box, taking care to 'stick' the landing.

Fig. 6.6 Counter movement jump.

Fig. 6.7 Vertical jump.

Fig. 6.8 Jumping up to box.

Fig. 6.8 (continued).

– It is important the chest remains high. The landing position should look like a technically sound, parallel squat position.

Concentric/Eccentric Coupling

The final piece of the plyometric jigsaw is to teach the ability to couple both concentric and eccentric movements together. It is this coupling and the ability to reduce the amortization phase (landing) in the middle that is fundamental to adaptations with the stretch shortening cycle. The basics of jumping and landing will take us a long way with untrained players. However, there comes a point where we must manipulate this coupling sequence to develop jump ability. Crucially, we must also increase the magnitude of the coupling response with 'shock' methods of jumping.

As a word of caution, many players may never be ready to get to these stages if the initial levels of strength, stability and coordination are not there. Remember to train what is in front of you. Some players will have the aptitude and athletic ability, some will not.

There is again scope to use a variety of exercises and drills to couple the concentric and eccentric actions together and as long as programming guidelines are followed the drill can be driven by the coach. Again, a simple approach will always bring about the best adaptations in most players as there will be little confusion or opportunity to work submaximally.

Cross drill

Drills such as this are a great warm-up to coupling and also a low level variant allowing athletes to strengthen the ankle musculature. The key is that the movements are precise but also carried out with sufficient intent.

Fig. 6.9 Double cross drill.

Fig. 6.10 Single cross drill.

- Use a marked cross on the floor or if you are on a track you can use the point where two lines cross.
- This will give four boxes that can be jumped in both as a double leg and single leg exercise.
- You should visualize a dot in each box and that is where you are going to land each time.
- Jump from one box to another making sure the landing and take-off are elastic and reactive. The player can move clockwise, anti-clockwise, laterally or forward and back. There is also the option to do this as a single leg exercise.

Toe taps

Toe taps can be done over small hurdles or without any apparatus at all. The key is that the movement comes from the lower leg, rather than flexing at the knee.

- Jump upwards, initiating the jump from the lower leg.
- The body should remain rigid, with the arms assisting in the propulsion of the body upwards. Have the player focus on a forceful contact with the ball of the foot through the floor and on attempting to get as much lift as possible.
- It is important that on the jump, the ankle and foot raise up to a dorsiflexion position. This pre-stretch allows the subsequent jump to be explosive as the action of the foot flexing down into the ground aids the explosive movement.

Fig. 6.11 Toe taps – double.

Fig. 6.11 (continued).

Depth jumps and 'Shock' variants

Depth jumps sit at the 'shock' end of the plyometric spectrum and usually do not find their way into programmes until later in the training journey. Owing to the increased force as players drop, the SSC must be used effectively to keep contact time to a minimum, thus using the stored energy. It can be beneficial to use two methods depending on the desired outcome and relation to game specific events.

- **Jump high:** By cueing the player to merely jump as high as possible we will see slightly longer contact times as he or she flexes down further. Although a slower plyometric jump, there is still a significant stretch load to tolerate and overcome
- **Jump high and jump fast:** The added cue of time dependency results in a faster plyometric jump but potentially lower jump heights. This jump involves a maximum

Fig. 6.12 Depth jumps.

Fig. 6.13 Depth jumps to box.

stretch load and is as intense a training movement as can be seen.

Rugby commonly has plyometric actions at the slower end of the spectrum but it is important to still train athletes to be effective through the whole force-velocity curve.

- The height of both boxes will be determined by the athlete's ability and previously mentioned heights should be used.
- Stand at the edge of the box with the foot pre-flexed
- Drop off the box, landing with the mid foot on the ground.
- On landing, jump reactively as high (or fast) as possible making sure the body extends fully through ankle, knee and hip.

Boxes or hurdles can be added on to the sequence to increase the difficulty. Once athletes are well developed with a strong and varied athletic skill set they will be able to be challenged more and will require greater stimuli to progress.

Programming Plyometrics Exercise

The programming of volume and intensity of plyometric activity should always be guided by a quality over quantity process. When done maximally (which is fundamental to using the SSC) there is a significant amount of neural recovery needed. Too often the drills can be rushed through, resulting in submaximal levels negating the possible benefits.

Plyometrics should be counted as a number of foot contacts in a session. A double leg or single leg landing will be counted as one contact. There will be a far greater fatiguing effect from coupling type exercises over landing and jumping. Three to five minutes should be allowed for full neural recovery with 48 to 72 hours between sessions.

Guidelines (1) suggest foot contacts for beginners to be 80–100, intermediate 100–120

and advanced 120–140 contacts. However, as a coach know your players; some can tolerate more, some less. Coach what you see in front of you and if the second form becomes poor, stop the drill.

It is also worth noting these standardized guidelines pay little attention to the intensity of a drill. Doing eighty contacts of 'shock' type plyometric drills such as depth jumps will take a far greater toll on the physical and neural systems than, say, eighty contacts of low level hops.

Linear Speed and Sprinting Mechanics

Speed wins games, whether it is pure speed, game speed or speed of execution. But it is an area that is often trained, rather than being coached, and as a result players seldom increase speed, they just become better at tolerating repeated exertions of the same speed. The correct coaching of linear running mechanics should cover two main areas:

- **Acceleration:** The ability of a player to go from nothing . . . to something. We are specifically looking at speeding up from a static/near static start or the ability to re-accelerate as part of agility,
- **Top Speed:** The ability of a player to have efficiency of movement at top speed and, crucially, have the skill, technique and musculature to recover the body, putting it in the best possible position to repeat the process.

While we take a model from track sprinting it is important coaches understand the crossover with rugby. Other than a player running the length of the field for an interception try, it is unlikely he or she will reach top speed and they will operate commonly at submaximal speeds of up to 70–80 per cent of their maximum speed. But if through a programmed approach to speed work we can increase maximal speed, submaximal speed has to improve as a result.

Acceleration: All players, regardless of position, are required to accelerate and, naturally, the better players are at this, the greater chance they will have of beating their opposite man. Underpinning the technical components below in acceleration coaching, a player is required to possess the four following qualities:

- **Posture:** The ability of a player to remain in an upright posturally sound position with 'high hips' will be central to the efficiency of the body to push force through the floor. If this postural integrity cannot be maintained as speed is increased we see the body 'break' in the mid section. This is no different to what occurs in players' gym-based exercise and thus parallels can be drawn from the two types of training. Creating and maintaining this rigid stability and posture throughout the whole chain of the body is fundamental to safe, efficient technique
- **Intent:** Speed is maximal. To accelerate players need to exert maximal intent. What you train for is what you get and, with acceleration, we are looking to coordinate the neuromuscular system so it not only activates. . . it does so quickly. This is a key consideration when coaching any speed type work. If players train fast and maximally they have a greater chance to become fast. In conjunction with a resistance programme we are looking to develop players' ability to create more force in the shortest possible time frame.
- **Joint stability:** Stiff, stretch resistant tendons aid the overall stability of the joint sites when sprinting. Energy can be lost at the ankle, knee, hip and shoulder joints predominantly if we have excessive instability and movement in the joints. Imagine a player accelerating from a

standing start. As he pushes into the floor to propel himself forwards, how much overall force he produces is irrelevant if the musculo-tendinous structures at the joints cannot transmit the force. Huge amounts of force are going through these structures and appropriate conditioning needs to be completed alongside technical work to guard against inefficient energy transfer. As a rule, if your players look unstable in static or low velocity, gym-based movements, they will definitely break down when velocity and intent are increased in sprinting.
- **Movement resistance:** Efficient technique at speed requires the body being able to withstand and resist significant movement. This is particularly the case with the mid section where excessive movement will result in reduced capacity for speed.

Coaching Acceleration

Provided we have a solid foundation in the qualities above we can look to develop drills to allow players to accelerate fast and aggressively. Think about what happens in acceleration. Players need the ability to exert explosive force, crucially in a concentric action. Provided the player is in a sound athletic position, that is flexed, all propulsive momentum will take him or her forwards through a concentric action. Crucially, this force needs to be applied as quickly as possible. Within the first two steps, a player will reach 50 per cent of top speed with an estimated 75 per cent reached within seven steps. So this start action and those first few steps are crucial if a player is to drive down and back into the ground efficiently. The legs should push up and down with short choppy steps in a piston-like fashion, beneath or behind the centre of mass. The player's body angle will be roughly 45 degrees, with a trajectory not unlike a plane on take-off. Fig. 6.14 outlines some of the key actions that occur.

Figure 6.14 Factors involved in acceleration.

Stride length and pattern	Short choppy steps to overcome the inertia of the stationary or slow moving, body. Looking for a piston-like action that takes us 'from nothing to something'
Foot contact (ground contact time)	Long drive out phase that involves the player 'pushing', leading to relatively long initial ground contact times
Body angle	Low to high trajectory with a forward. There is a positive 45 degree shin angle. Visualize a plane taking off
Speed	50% speed reached in two steps. 75% reached in seven steps. 80-85% reached by 20m
Frequency	Slow initially with a low heel recovery. However, the intent should be to pump the legs as fast as possible

It is effective to coach acceleration in an upright position initially to groove in technique, progressing later to wall drills (thus bringing the body angle closer to true acceleration) and finally to a variety of start positions. While the arms are vital to assist propulsion, initially players can find it complicated to concentrate too much on arm technique. However, it must be stressed most of the movement comes from the shoulder joint and not the elbow. Players will often think flexing and extending the arms with repeated velocity at the elbow signifies speed but in effect it is just wasting energy. Big powerful arms should be driven by the shoulder and, crucially, the right arm should move with the left leg, and vice versa.

High knee walk

Fig. 6.15 High knee walk.

The high knee walk is the base skill and body position for all subsequent acceleration work.
- Chest is held high with good posture in a 'tall hips' position. This posture must be maintained throughout.
- The support leg is straight with the hips extended fully through.
- The opposite leg comes up to 90 degrees, crucially with the foot dorsiflexed. This allows the foot to drive down through the floor when the speed of the drills is increased. If the toes were to point downward it would result in ground contact being a pawing action.

138

- The player should concentrate on opposite arm and leg chains of movement with the arm driving from the shoulder. The fingers travel from 'hip to lip'.
- The player should alternate this position, walking while maintaining a good technical position. The drill is done with a flat foot contact.

Dynamic high knee walk

Fig. 6.16 Dynamic high knee walk.

The technical points of the dynamic high knee walk are the same as above but there is a greater intent and force in the movement. This results in the player driving up on to the mid foot. As the speed increases, the coach should make sure good posture and a fully extended hip position is maintained.

High knee skip

Fig. 6.17 High knee skip.

- Progressing from the dynamic high knee walk, the skip looks to increase again how much force is pushed into the floor.
- The speed at which one leg goes up is dictated by the speed by which the other drives down into the floor and coaching cues should look to achieve this.
- The heel of the support leg should never make contact with the floor. Coaches talk about a credit card distance from the floor, the idea being that the heel will always act as a brake, the ball of the foot an accelerator.
- As a result, we see a much more piston-like movement now with the legs driving up and down into the floor.

Toe tap doubles

We have highlighted the need to maintain stiffness through the joint sites in order not to dissipate energy. Once a player can achieve an upright acceleration position we need to introduce ankle stiffness drills. If a player is to drive out aggressively and not collapse at the ankle he or she must have both the range of motion and the ability to use the ankle to contact with the floor.

– The body should be in a rigid extended posture with the player initiating all movement from the lower leg.

– As the player jumps, the ankle joint should move from a plantar flexed (toes down) to a dorsiflexed position (toes up).
– The reverse then occurs on the way down so the ball of the foot can make contact with the ground.
– The player should attempt to push the floor away aggressively on contact, causing him or her to lift again.
– The drill should occur with a bouncy, vertical lift on each contact and there should be a relaxed rhythmical pattern.

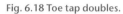

Fig. 6.18 Toe tap doubles.

Fig. 6.18 (continued).

Toe tap singles
To progress the drill, a player then applies the same concept but alternating with single contacts.

Bounce, bounce, switch
The final piece of the jigsaw, as it were, is to add knee lift drills with ankle stiffness drills. This also helps develop the complex coordinated movement sequence of sprinting and develops both rhythm and neural sequencing.
– Start in the initial high knee walk position.
– Bounce twice on the support leg, concentrating on stiffness in the ankle and a vertical lift.
– After the two bounces players should switch legs aggressively and repeat.
– The drill should be coached so a player achieves a high level of foot contacts, rather than horizontal speed being the goal.

Fig. 6.19 Toe tap singles.

Fig. 6.19 (continued).

Using a wall gives an opportunity for us to take the upright acceleration mechanics down to an angle that is closer to a true acceleration 'low to high' position.

- Stand in the high knee position and fall forwards so the wall supports the body.
- The forward position means a player needs to hold sound postural mechanics and remain fully extended through the hips.
- The player should drive the leg down into the floor coinciding with the support leg rising up to the high knee position. This mimics the action of the high knee drills.
- The player should start with single repetitions, building to sets of alternate repetitions.

Wall start
- The player will start from the floor in a sprint start position.
- The heel of the forward leg should align with the knee of the trailing leg.

Wall drive

Fig. 6.20 Wall drive.

Fig. 6.21 Wall start.

Fig. 6.21 (continued).

– From the start position, the player drives upwards into the wall. This powerful concentric drive means the player ends up in the start position of the wall drive drill.

Falling start
– The final sequence to take the player into true acceleration is to put the body into a 'falling' forward lean position.
– The player holds a high knee position and extends up on to the ball of the foot.
– Falling forward, the player should drive the foot down into the ground and push back to propel himself or herself forward.
– The player will self-select how far he or she falls forward based on ability and over time they should look to fall to a position of roughly 45 degrees.

Fig. 6.22 Falling start.

Fig. 6.22 (continued).

Coaching Top Speed

Maximal top speed in rugby tends not to occur too much because of the confines of the game but there is still merit in its coaching. Running efficiently requires a significant neural component that allows a player to produce some repeated coordinate movements. This development of motor skill and the overall physical benefits of top speed running, specifically in hamstring conditioning and joint structure conditioning, means it should always find its way into a player's physical work programme. Its inclusion is questioned at times, largely due to the lack of actual top speed running in rugby, with submaximal game speed of around 60–80 per cent more common. However, if the top speed is increased, submaximal speed will always increase as a result and thus its training has merit.

A cyclical action, as opposed to the piston-like mechanics of acceleration posture, is still central to an efficient technique. Crucially though, being able to step over the knee (and driving down) and having a high heel recovery at speed means players should transfer force running across the ground, as opposed to driving through it. Fig. 6.23 shows the key technical points of top speed running.

Heel to bottom (walking, backwards, running)

– Have players imagine they are drawing a line up the support leg with the ankle of the other leg.
– The posture does not differ from any of the other drills and players with compromised hip mobility and stability may struggle.
– Walk up the track alternating leg per step working to keep the heel tight to the buttock.
– Players can start by walking forwards and then trying the same action backwards. The final progression is into running action, with heel going to bottom.

Figure 6.23 Factors involved with top speed running.

Stride length and pattern	Increased stride length, as opposed to acceleration, resembling a cyclical motion. While acceleration is concerned with front side action, top speed relates more to backside recovery mechanics
Foot contact (ground contact time)	At top speed ground contact is reduced with the player appearing to run over the surface
Body angle	The body becomes more upright with a tall posture and 'high hips', the shin angle moved from a positive angle to a more neutral one
Speed	Maximum speed can be reached by 60m, after which it is more the player's ability to maintain speed
Frequency	Frequency builds initially then it maintains by stepping over the knee

Fig. 6.24 Heel to bottom.

Fig. 6.24 (continued).

Fig. 6.25 Wall cycle.

Wall cycle

– The player starts in the standard high knee position, supported by the wall.
– The player should drive the foot down and back rapidly, allowing the foot to drag past the support leg.
– The recovery phase has a high heel recovery in a cyclical action with the heel moving up over the knee and to the bottom.

Fig. 6.26 Step over shin.

Step over shin/knee
- Once a player masters the cyclical recovery of the wall cycle he or she can look to use it while moving.
- Start initially with the player stepping over the mid shin, progressing to the knee.
- It can help to have the player visualize squashing a box in front of him or her, emphasizing the need for the mid foot to push down and back.
- The leg then recovers at the desired height, progressing to stepping over the knee.

Fig. 6.27 Step over knee.

With all acceleration on top speed technique drills we follow the 'slow to fast' guideline for progression. Although players can often take time to perfect the drills, they benefit from considerable adaptations both structurally and neutrally and from an injury prevention perspective. As players develop, look to follow:

- Acceleration drill into stride out
- Top speed drill into stride out
- Acceleration drill into top speed drill
- Acceleration drill into top speed drill into stride out
- Maximal work.

Coaching Agility and Game Speed

Alongside a solid coaching focus on linear speed, rugby will always need to allocate time to the development of game speed, the ability of a player to reduce speed and re-accelerate in a number of different directions. Through a combination of physical skills and technical sports skills players will develop a multi-directional skill set to speed that, in a game scenario, will give them tactical and physical options to better their opposition. For players to make the right movement at the right time, and crucially do it quicker than the opposition players, they require not only the decision-making ability and motor skill but also:

- **Relative strength:** Players who cannot deal with their own body mass through their relative strength will always be at a disadvantage. Overall strength, specifically in multi-directional patterns and on one leg, will dominate. Likewise, because of the high eccentric component in deceleration, force reduction and position postural management need to be addressed.

- **Speed:** Overall acceleration and top speed will determine the speeds a player is capable of in a game. We previously discussed the concept of increasing the type of submaximal speed that occurs in game scenarios. Agility is acceleration-based in that it often entails going from 'something to nothing', or 'something to something faster'.
- **Motor coordination:** A player needs the physical characteristics but must train the efficient neural pathways that facilitate complex movement.
- **Stability:** Both on a technical proficiency level and in the player's ability to control his or her centre of gravity, they must be stable. Strength programmes focusing on anti-rotation/flexion/extension cross over well to controlling the body at speed. Controlling the base of support in a player's mechanics is an important part of efficient agility.
- **Technique:** Specifically, control around the ankle, knee, hip and trunk alignment allows the player to make the right movement at the right time.
- **Flexibility/mobility:** Owing to the multiplanar nature of agility and the increased ranges a player must deal with, comprehensive movement competency is essential.
- **Anaerobic conditioning:** The repeated nature in rugby of these events means sufficient work capacity must be built in order for a player to be at a high standard for the full 80 minutes.

When selecting agility drills and exercises, it is important to ensure two main tenets exist rather than trying to devise complicated drills. Learning the basic techniques and then applying them to progressive drills, aligned with a structured strength programme, will always produce superior results. We are looking for a player to produce greater levels of force into the ground, in shorter possible time frames and in multi-directional planes. However, without also developing the ability to slow down or reduce force as quickly as possible, a player will be one dimensional.

To a degree, a player's capacity for speed and agility is in part genetics and thus something a coach cannot change. Anthropometry, fibre type and general mentality in terms of decision-making are not likely to be influenced in sessions. However, there are several areas that can be impacted. Fig 6.28 shows both kinetic factors that are trainable and kinematic factors that are coachable. As an effective coach it is important to understand what fits where and which approach is needed.

Sprint stop drill
While the drill selection is at the discretion of the host, the ability to slow down will be

Trainable – Kinetic Variables	Coachable – Kinematic variables
Force production	Angular, postural position of the body
Impulse and intent	How the player controls the centre of mass
Movement	How the player controls the base of support
Power	
Structural compliance	
Tendon stiffness	

Fig. 6.28 Trainable kinetic variables and coachable kinematic variables.

integral to all drills so it is perhaps the main skill to teach. Once perfected, drills can follow the standard progressions of closed drills into open drills, simple into complex and slow into fast.

- Have the player accelerate hard on a 15–20m shuttle that has a line marked at the end.
- The player should accelerate as hard as possible and should look to stop as late as possible. We want the player to be able to stop dead on the second line, in an athletic 'ready to go' position.
- If acceleration has been taught well, then slowing down should be a mirror image.
- In order to slow down, a player must come from a high to a low position, lowering the centre of gravity.
- Body weight shifts back into the heels allowing a wider base of support and increases in friction, aiding slowing down.
- Vision should be straight ahead with the player coming to a stop in an 'athletic position'. Weight is loaded in the mid foot with ankle, knee and hip flexed, meaning the player can move in any other direction.

As a progression a player should:

- Sprint stop forwards and back
- Sprint stop laterally
- Undertake arcing and figure-of-eight type drills
- Carry out sprint-stop-sprint variations in multiple directions.

Programming of Speed, Agility and Plyometrics

Coaches should always follow a process of quality over quantity for all speed and plyometric training. Players need to first build sound technique through drills but then, most importantly, the movements must be done maximally. If players only ever sprint at 80 per cent of top speed, for example, they basically only ever get better at running at submaximal speed.

Rugby has often looked at games as a method of speed development, or training speed at the end of technical sessions, which has resulted in players either trying to develop speed in a fatigued state or in poor body positions. The coach has to coordinate with technical coaches the optimal time for speed work if it is to have success. You get players faster by increasing their production of peak force and producing it in a short time, meaning both speed work and gym-based resistance programmes need to be implemented.

Sample acceleration session
Remember the two key concepts – posture and maximal intent:

Walking high knee	3 × 20m
Dynamic high knee	3 × 20m
High knee run	3 × 10m
Ankle tap doubles	3 × 10m
Ankle tap singles	3 × 10m
Bounce, bounce, switch	3 × 20m
Wall drive (single efforts)	2 × 8 each side

Mode	Work Duration	Rest Duration	Work: Rest
Speed/agility	<6sec	>2min	1:20
Speed endurance	6-30sec	2-10min	1:20
Repeated sprint	<10sec	50-80sec	1:5-1:8
Speed/anaerobic	10-20sec	30-60sec	1:3

Figure 6.29 Work: rest durations for plyometrics, speed and agility.

Wall drive (repeated
   efforts) ....3 × 12 alternating
Crouching sprint start .... 4 × 20m
Kneeling sprint start........................... 4 × 20m
Chest flat start .... 2 × 20m

Sample max speed drills
Remember the concepts of a cyclical action with good recovery of the leg. A selection of standard acceleration drills can be implemented into the warm-up:
Wall cycle .... 2 × 10 each side
Stepping over (shin) .... 3 × 20m
Stepping over (knee) .... 3 × 20m
Walking heel to bottom (foward)....... 3 × 20m
Walking heel to bottom (back) .... 3 × 20m
Running heel to bottom .... 3 × 20m
Acceleration into top speed
   stride...................................... 5 × 20m>30m

Sample agility session
Remember to control the centre of mass. Keep low. A selection of standard acceleration and top speed drills can be implemented in the warm-up:

Drop and stick .... 3 × 5
Hop and hold .... 2 × 5 each
Hop and hold lateral....................... 2 × 5 each
Sprint stop (feet parallel) .... 5 × 10m
Sprint stop (feet split) .... 6 × 10m
Sprint stop sprint (use a variety of
   direction changes)......................... 5 × 10m
Slow/fast/slow .... 4 × 10m/10m/10m
Fast/slow/fast................... 4 × 10m/10m/10m

REFERENCES

Chapter 1

1. Faigenbaum, A. D., Kraemer, W. J., Cahill, B., Chandler, J., Dziados, J., Elfrink, L. D. & Roberts, S. (1996). Youth Resistance Training: Position Statement Paper and Literature Review: Position Statement. *Strength & Conditioning Journal, 18* (6), pp.62–76.

2. Quarrie, K. L., Gianotti, S. M., Hopkins, W. G., & Hume, P. A. (2007). Effect of nationwide injury prevention programme on serious spinal injuries in New Zealand rugby union: ecological study. *bmj, 334* (7604), p.1150.

3. Roberts, S. P., Trewartha, G., Higgitt, R. J., El-Abd, J., & Stokes, K. A. (2008). The physical demands of elite English rugby union. *Journal of Sports Sciences, 26* (8), pp.825–833.

4. McMahon, S., & Wenger, H. A. (1998). The relationship between aerobic fitness and both power output and subsequent recovery during maximal intermittent exercise. *Journal of Science and Medicine in Sport, 1* (4), pp.219–227.

5. Duthie, G., Pyne, D., & Hooper, S. (2003). Applied physiology and game analysis of rugby union. *Sports Medicine, 33* (13), pp.973–991.

6. Deutsch, M. U., Kearney, G. A., & Rehrer, N. J. (2007). Time–motion analysis of professional rugby union players during match-play. *Journal of Sports Sciences, 25* (4), pp.461–472.

7. *Essentials of strength training and conditioning.* Vol. 7. Champaign, IL: Human kinetics, 2008.

8. Stone, M. H., Stone, M., Sands, W. A., & Sands, B. (2007). *Principles and practice of resistance training.* Human Kinetics.

9. Clark, M., Lucett, S., & Kirkendall, D. T. (2010). *NASM's essentials of sports performance training.* Lippincott Williams & Wilkins.

10. Aagaard, P., Simonsen, E. B., Andersen, J. L., Magnusson, P., & Dyhre-Poulsen, P. (2002). Increased rate of force development and neural drive of human skeletal muscle following resistance training. *Journal of Applied Physiology, 93* (4), pp.1318–1326.

11. Harman, E. (1994). Resistance training modes: A biomechanical perspective. *Strength & Conditioning Journal, 16* (2), pp.59–65.

12. Cardinale, M., Newton, R., & Nosaka, K. (Eds.) (2011). *Strength and conditioning: biological principles and practical applications.* John Wiley & Sons.

13. Bruce, S. A., Phillips, S. K., & Woledge, R. C. (1997). Interpreting the relation between force and cross-sectional area in human muscle. *Medicine and Science in Sports and Exercise, 29* (5), pp.677–683.

Chapter 2

1. Selye, H. (1936). The Alarm Reaction, *Canadian Medical Association Journal, 34,* p.706.
2. Verkhoshansky, Y. V. (1985). Programming and organization of the training process Publishing house 'Physical Culture and Sport'.
3. Siff, M. C., & Verkhoshansky, Y. V. (2004). *Supertraining.* Supertraining Institute.

Chapter 3

1. Lloyd, R. S., Oliver, J. L., Meyers, R. W., Moody, J. A., & Stone, M. H. (2012). Long-term athletic development and its application to youth weightlifting. *Strength & Conditioning Journal, 34* (4), pp.55–66.
2. Lloyd, R. S., Faigenbaum, A. D., Myer, G. D., Stone, M. H., Oliver, J. L., Jeffreys, I., Moody, J., Brewer, C., & Pierce, K. (2012). UKSCA position statement: Youth resistance training. *Professional Strength and Conditioning, 26,* pp.26–39.
3. Balyi, I., & Hamilton, A. (2004). Long-term athlete development: trainability in childhood and adolescence. *Olympic Coach, 16* (1), pp.4–9.
4. Lloyd, R. S., & Oliver, J. L. (2012). The youth physical development model: A new approach to long-term athletic development. *Strength & Conditioning Journal, 34* (3), pp.61–72.
5. Rogol, A. D., Clark, P. A., & Roemmich, J. N. (2000). Growth and pubertal development in children and adolescents: effects of diet and physical activity. *The American Journal of Clinical Nutrition, 72* (2), pp.521s–528s.
6. Myer, G. D., Ford, K. R., Palumbo, O. P., & Hewett, T. E. (2005). Neuromuscular training improves performance and lower-extremity biomechanics in female athletes. *The Journal of Strength & Conditioning Research, 19* (1), pp.51–60.
7. McLeod, T. C. V., Decoster, L. C., Loud, K. J., Micheli, L. J., Parker, J. T., Sandrey, M. A., & White, C. (2011). National Athletic Trainers' Association position statement: prevention of pediatric overuse injuries. *Journal of Athletic Training, 46* (2), p.206.
8. MacKelvie, K. J., Khan, K. M., & McKay, H. A. (2002). Is there a critical period for bone response to weight-bearing exercise in children and adolescents? A systematic review. *British Journal of Sports Medicine, 36* (4), pp.250–257.
9. Faigenbaum, A. D., Kraemer, W. J., Blimkie, C. J., Jeffreys, I., Micheli, L. J., Nitka, M., & Rowland, T. W. (2009). Youth resistance training: updated position statement paper from the National Strength and Conditioning Association. *The Journal of Strength & Conditioning Research, 23,* S60–S79.
10. Javorek, I. S. (1998). The benefits of combination lifts. *Strength & Conditioning Journal, 20* (3), pp.53–57.

Chapter 5

1. Baker, D. (2001). A series of studies on the training of high-intensity muscle power in rugby league football players. *The Journal of Strength & Conditioning Research, 15* (2), pp.198–209.
2. Baker, D. (2001). Acute and long-term power responses to power training: Observations on the training of an elite power athlete. *Strength & Conditioning Journal, 23* (1), pp.47–56.
3. Baker, D. (2003). Acute effect of alternating heavy and light resistances on power output during upper-body complex power training. *The Journal of Strength & Conditioning Research, 17* (3), pp.493–497.

4. Siff, M. C., & Verkhoshansky, Y. V. (2004). *Supertraining*. Supertraining Institute.

5. Dan Baker in Joyce, D., & Lewindon, D. (Eds.) (2014). *High-Performance Training for Sports*. Human Kinetics.

6. Baker, D., & Nance, S. (1999). The relation between running speed and measures of strength and power in professional rugby league players. *The Journal of Strength & Conditioning Research, 13* (3), pp.230–235.

7. Stone, M. H., Stone, M., Sands, W. A., & Sands, B. (2007). *Principles and practice of resistance training*. Human Kinetics.

8. Young, W. B., Jenner, A., & Griffiths, K. (1998). Acute enhancement of power performance from heavy load squats. *The Journal of Strength & Conditioning Research, 12* (2), pp.82–84.

9. Wisløff, U., Castagna, C., Helgerud, J., Jones, R., & Hoff, J. (2004). Strong correlation of maximal squat strength with sprint performance and vertical jump height in elite soccer players. *British Journal of Sports Medicine, 38* (3), pp.285–288.

10. Carlock, J. M., Smith, S. L., Hartman, M. J., Morris, R. T., Ciroslan, D. A., Pierce, K. C., & Stone, M. H. (2004). The relationship between vertical jump power estimates and weightlifting ability: a field-test approach. *The Journal of Strength & Conditioning Research, 18* (3), p.534–539.

11. Cormie, P., McGuigan, M. R., & Newton, R. U. (2010). Adaptations in athletic performance after ballistic power versus strength training. *Med Sci Sports Exerc, 42*(8), pp.1582–1598.

12. Cormie, P., McCaulley, G. O., Triplett, N. T., & McBride, J. M. (2007). Optimal loading for maximal power output during lower-body resistance exercises. *Medicine and Science in Sports and Exercise, 39* (2), p.340.

13. Hameed, M., Orrell, R. W., Cobbold, M., Goldspink, G., & Harridge, S. D. R. (2003). Expression of IGF-I splice variants in young and old human skeletal muscle after high resistance exercise. *The Journal of Physiology, 547* (1), pp.247–254.

14. Haff, G. G., & Nimphius, S. (2012). Training principles for power. *Strength & Conditioning Journal, 34* (6), pp.2–12.

15. Aagaard, P., Simonsen, E. B., Andersen, J. L., Magnusson, P., & Dyhre-Poulsen, P. (2002). Increased rate of force development and neural drive of human skeletal muscle following resistance training. *Journal of Applied Physiology, 93* (4), pp.1318–1326.

16. Gambetta, V., & Clark, M. (1999). Hard core training. *Training and Conditioning, 9* (4), pp.34–40.

Chapter 6

1. *Essentials of strength training and conditioning*. Vol. 7. Champaign, IL: Human kinetics, 2008

INDEX

ABOUT THE AUTHOR

During a ten-year professional career Joel Brannigan played for clubs such as Edinburgh Rugby, London Welsh and Newcastle Falcons. His representative honours saw him play for Scotland at full international level and various lower representative levels. Following retirement in 2004 he pursued a career in the field of strength and conditioning and spent eight years as head of strength and conditioning at the University of Northumbria, working with a wide range of sports and athletes from Olympic level down to recreational student athletes. Currently he works as a strength and conditioning coach with Durham County Cricket Club.

Holding an MSc in strength and conditioning, he is also employed by the United Kingdom Strength and Conditioning Association as a tutor and assessor on its accreditation process. Within rugby he has delivered to professional players, 'age grade' representative players and recreational rugby players. He has a strong interest in rugby at all levels but specifically the development of junior level players.

RELATED TITLES FROM CROWOOD

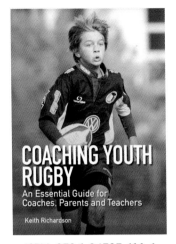

ISBN: 978 1 84797 611 6

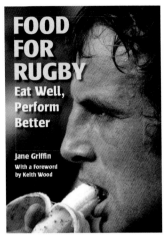

ISBN: 978 1 86126 695 8

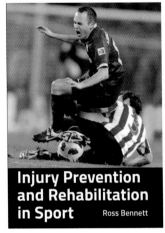

ISBN: 978 1 84797 957 5

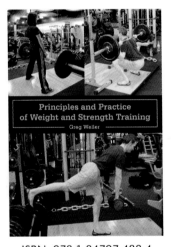

ISBN: 978 1 84797 488 4

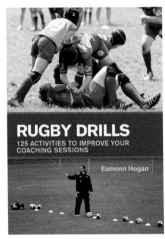

ISBN: 978 1 84797 655 0

ISBN: 978 1 86126 850 1

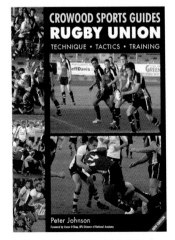

ISBN: 978 1 84797 064 0

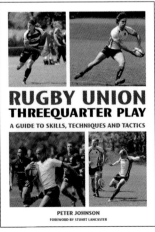

ISBN: 978 1 84797 395 5

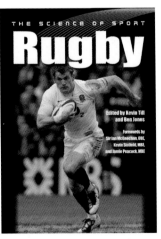

ISBN: 978 1 78500 106 2